One
for sorrow
two for joy

MARY COOK

One for sorrow two for joy

DENEAU

Published by Deneau Publishers
411 Queen Street, Ottawa, Canada K1R 5A6

©Mary Cook 1984
Printed and bound in Canada by John Deyell Company
First printing 1984

Editor: Barbara Stevenson
Cover design: Heather Walters
Painting: *Fairy Tales* by Mary Bell Eastlake
Reproduced courtesy of Mrs. Archer N. Budden and
The National Gallery of Canada

Canadian Cataloguing in Publication Data
Cook, Mary, 1932-
One for sorrow, two for joy
ISBN 0-88879-110-0
1. Cook, Mary, 1932- 2. Farm life — Ottawa River Valley
(Quebec and Ont.) 3. Ottawa River Valley (Quebec and
Ont.) — History
I. Title
FC 3095.R4C65 1984 971.3'803'0924 C84-090135-6
F1059.R4C65 1984

iv

One for sorrow, two for joy,
Three for a girl, four for a boy,
Five for silver, six for gold,
Seven for a secret ne'er to be told.

Contents

INTRODUCTION

I t seems now, so many years later, that even though our parents worried through the depression years, our lives as children were filled with joy and contentment. The memories are ones of cozy feather-filled beds, evening sing-songs, abundant tables and a loving family.

Mother was the force to be reckoned with in our family — strong, willful and devoted to her home and children. Father, quiet and hardworking, slow to anger and of solid German background, in many ways complemented my mother's volatile French Canadian nature.

My older sister, Audrey, seemed very clever to me. She could sing on tune, braid long grass and would put a protective arm around me whenever I needed it. My three brothers were very different. Everett, the oldest, was very much like Father while the youngest, Earl, was small, artistic and dutiful. Emerson, the middle one, gained notoriety in the family album where he was recorded as coming into the world weighing a whopping 14 pounds and 11½ ounces.

Two cousins from Montreal spent several months each year on the farm with us and were almost like brothers. Ronny, the eldest, was a terror and, at an early age, earned the reputation of being completely incorrigible. His younger brother, Terry, was a golden-haired angel by comparison. Although considered delicate, he soon grew into a healthy, robust adolescent. Their early years were so intertwined with ours that I can scarcely recall a time when they weren't there.

Renfrew County, where most of the stories originate, was like any other rural community during the depression. The people were honest, hardworking, funloving and God-fearing. They sealed contracts with the shake of a hand, and heaven help the man who didn't keep his word.

One for Sorrow, Two for Joy is a collection of stories about those years in the thirties when I grew up as the youngest child in a warm, close-knit farm family. Some of the people are real; some exist only in my imagination. And while some of the stories are based on actual events, others come from "mind-the-time" exchanges at family gatherings or from my mother's remembrances.

The stories could have happened anywhere — they are really memories of an era rather than an area — and I hope, for each one told, readers will be able to recall one of their own.

MOTHER AND THE FIELD MICE

O ur mother was an imposing figure, tall and broad-shouldered, with a no-nonsense walk that had people turning their heads on the Renfrew streets when she passed by. She'd tackle any chore on the farm. She could run the thrashing machine as well as Father, swill the pigs, deliver a calf and shovel manure with the best of them. But there was one thing that reduced her to a quivering coward, and that was the sight of a mouse.

She didn't like mouse traps either and that was a problem. She said the snap of the traps in the middle of the night meant that one of the little creatures had been scurrying through the house before its capture, and goodness knows what dish it had run over in the cupboard beforehand. No, if there was a mouse about, she preferred not to know it.

Field mice came into the old log house through many avenues — doors that did not shut tightly, the back summer kitchen where you could put your hand through the boards in some places and the chimney which connected to a net-work of pipes that snaked through the house. It was almost impossible to make the house mouseproof, although, good-ness knows, Mother tried. She packed cloth around holes at the baseboards and nailed pieces of shingles to every little opening she saw in the floor. She would not allow the small-est crumb to fall to the floor without running for the broom and dustpan, just in case a mouse could smell it from the

3

outside walls. She did everything in her power to keep the field mice outside but occasionally, in spite of her valiant efforts, one of the little grey sleek-bodied creatures would find its way in.

We learned early in the game not to let on if we saw a mouse scurrying along the baseboards, but Mother seemed to have a special radar system. She was known to turn around completely in her chair and scream, "There's a mouse behind the stove." We never knew how she sensed it, but she did. Whenever she laid eyes on one, the trouble began. She would jump onto the nearest chair and we'd fly into action like a well-drilled battalion. Although we put on a good show, we inwardly hoped our blows would never connect as we went through the house slamming mop, broom and yardstick against the walls and furniture. Father thought it was lunacy not to set a trap and have the thing done and finished with, and he refused to take part in what he called a show better than anything you'd see at the Renfrew Fair. He would either quit the house entirely, or prop himself on a chair tilted back against the wainscotting and puff madly on his pipe, rooting for the mouse under his breath.

Emerson loved the drama of the whole performance, and he had no intention of ever swatting the mouse and sending it into oblivion. He preferred to trap it in some remote corner of a room, catch it by the tail and carry it squealing to the door to release it far from the house. He always made sure Mother was well aware he had caught it by carrying it past her and dangling its gyrating body close to her chair. At that point, she would be shouting to remove it immediately to the outdoors, and take it at least as far as the silo — preferably releasing it close to one of the big hungry barn cats who would finish it off for good.

As soon as the mouse was out of the house, Mother would jump off the chair and immediately become the self reliant, strong, capable individual we knew. It would be as if the fiasco never happened. She never apologized for her weakness — she loathed mice, was terrified of them and had no intention of changing.

It always amazed my sister and me, and we discussed it at great length when we were alone in our bedroom, how this strong, tall woman with the impressive ability to command couldn't cope with something as harmless as a field mouse.

⌬ATHER'S FLOWERS

M y father was a man who showed little emotion. The only way we could tell he was angry was through the twitching of his pipe. When he was pleased or happy, a quick smile would surface at one corner of his mouth, but it would be gone before it got used to being there, as my mother used to say.

However, when it came to flowers and plants, my father became a different person. He talked to his flowers long before it was fashionable to do so and, in a community where it was considered frivolous to have flower gardens in the yard, we had a profusion of rainbow colours from early summer until fall.

Every window sill inside the house held little baking powder cans or honey pails filled with house plants. We were never allowed to throw out a tin from the kitchen. They were washed and put in the car shed and, when Father needed one for a new cutting, he would punch holes in the bottom with a spike, another saucer from the kitchen cupboard would vanish, and a new plant would be crammed onto the already bulging window sills.

Often we would hear Father talking out on the back step in low hushed tones, and we knew he would be caressing his flowers with words. "Well, how are you today little redhead," he would say to a geranium, or "hello, bright eyes," to the daisies.

Since we grew up with this idiosyncrasy, we never thought it odd. And way back then, Father insisted the reason his flowers did so well was because they responded to the sound of his voice. Certainly the profusion of colour would attest to the fact that there was more truth than poetry in his philosophy.

It was an embarrassment to Mother when Father, while driving through town, would grind the old Ford to a halt in front of the house of a perfect stranger, leap out of the car, rap on the door and ask if he could have a cutting off a flower in the front yard. He was never refused, but I'm sure people wondered about the farmer in the weather-beaten straw hat, homemade plaid shirt, bib overalls and gum-rubbers asking for something as fragile as a cutting from a plant.

He had no special plan for planting his flowers. He put them wherever he found a good spot. We had no flower beds as such, but rather the tiger lilies grew around the smoke house because Father insisted they responded to the smell of the hemlock, the daisies were near the ice house because they liked the late day shade and the snapdragons were close to the pump because Father watered them every day.

I don't recall that anyone had lawn-mowers in those days — we used a scythe to cut the grass in the yard — and one day Father announced that it was Emerson's turn to make the front lawn look ''daycent,'' as he called it.

Emerson knew only one way to do a job, and that was in a hurry so that he could move on to better things like swimming in the Bonnechere River or playing ball at Thoms on the next farm. He tackled the lawn with a vengeance and was finished in jig-time, raking the grass and putting it in a heap at the back of the house where it was allowed to dry out before we burned it.

Father came in at noon to inspect the job and, for a man who showed little emotion, let out a great roar from the back of the house. Mother dropped the potato pot onto the back of the stove, and we children hurriedly dried our hands on the roller towel and tore out the back door to see what had happened.

There was Father, jumping straight up and down. His pipe had fallen to the ground, and he looked like he was ready to kill. Between what we all knew was German cussing, we heard bits and snatches of words which we soon realized had something to do with the mound of grass in front of him. We stood and watched until the tirade ended and, when he was completely calm, he got down on one knee and passed his hand over what he said were his very favourite flowers. Emerson had scythed them off at the roots. I don't think he would have been more upset if one of his children had fallen out of a tree and broken a limb. But there was nothing to do now but survey the damage.

Ever after, when the grass had to be scythed, Father sat on the back step and never took his eyes off the blade. If we came within a foot of one of his flowers, he let out a roar which could be heard in the next county.

OF MICE AND GINGERBREAD MEN

C hristmas baking was a special tradition when I was growing up on the farm, and it involved all of the children.
It made no difference to Mother that three of the five children were boys — they, too, donned the big white flour bag
pinnies and set to the task. Mother, who helped us as little
as possible with the actual baking, let us choose whatever
we wanted to make.

I always made gingerbread men. We had an old-fashioned
cookie cutter and, when the little men were baked, I loved
to decorate them with soft icing sugar which I coloured in
bright red and green. Emerson, whose one mission in life
was to aggravate me to tears, decided on an elaborate cake
that he had found the recipe for in Mother's old *Boston Cook
Book*. Mother cautioned him that it was an intricate recipe
demanding a lot of concentration and elbow grease, but he
was not to be discouraged — the four-tiered cake it was going
to be.

We were all spread out around the big pine table in the
kitchen, and Mother circled around, giving advice here and
a comment there, but never really interfering with our Christmas baking. "Beat harder, Emerson," she said a couple of
times. Emerson's reply was, "It'll make no difference when
it hits the oven." "Yes, it will," she said, but Emerson —
as arrogant as his twelve years would allow — assured her
he was doing just fine.

9

My gingerbread cookies were beautiful. They came from the oven perfectly shaped and, when they cooled down, I started the job I loved most — putting icing buttons and smiling faces on each one. Emerson had drawn a chair up to the oven to keep a close eye on his masterpiece, as he began to call it, scowling in the direction of my gingerbread men. He pulled a straw from the broom, opened the oven door and there, inside, were the flattest round cakes I had ever seen. They hadn't risen more than half an inch, and the straw came out nice and clean, so they were well-cooked.

I secretly gloated. When he had the layers iced, the entire cake was no more than two inches high. Emerson insisted that was the way it was supposed to be, but the rest of us said it was the tiredest looking cake we'd ever seen. Mother suggested we could use his cake with a sauce. Audrey suggested it would be great added to the pig feed. Emerson was getting more furious by the minute.

When we finished our baking, it was the custom to put it out in the back kitchen to freeze, to be brought in as needed. Emerson put the cake in a large, brown paper bag and carted it out to the old table. My cookies had already been spread out on two flat cookie sheets, and a clean tea towel covered them. When they were frozen solid, I would do as I always did — put them into a cookie tin and bring them out on Christmas Eve, leaving one out for Santa on the kitchen table.

When I got up the next morning, I rushed to the back kitchen and felt the frosty air on my bare arms. It was a good night for freezing, and the cookies would be ready to pack away. I lifted the tea towel and there, right before my eyes, were two dozen headless gingerbread men. Every last one of them was mutilated at the shoulders. I roared into the kitchen, screaming all the way.

Emerson denied having anything to do with the dastardly deed and said he'd bet his last cent that a mouse had gone at them. Audrey, who was mighty suspicious of the whole thing, said "And I suppose they just liked the heads?" "It looks like it," said Emerson calmly between mouthfuls of porridge.

Well, you couldn't punish someone for something he wouldn't own up to. I went off to school furious and refused to walk with Emerson, keeping about 100 yards behind him all the way. There was certainly no doubt in my mind what had happened to my gingerbread men.

That night when I came home there was a new batch of cookie dough ready for me, and in jig-time I had twenty-four little gingerbread men lined up on the cookie sheets. This time, Mother stored them in her big turkey roaster until they were frozen and ready to transfer to cookie tins.

As she carried the roaster out to the back kitchen, she cast a withering look at Emerson, who was watching the procedure from the back stairwell. When she went through the door, she turned to give him another glare, slapped the top lid of the roaster a couple of times with her hand and slowly, to leave a lasting impression, said, "Now let's see the mice get into this batch."

THE FAMILY PORTRAIT

T he ad in the *Renfrew Mercury* said simply, "family por-
traits — two dollars — one day only at the Renfrew
Hotel." Mother broached the subject to Father who thought
it was the most extravagant idea he had ever heard of, but
allowed that if she could come up with the two dollars, there
was no reason why we couldn't have a family picture taken.
Surprising all of us, she went to the emergency tea pot in
the cupboard and counted out the exact change. We didn't
even have to kill any chickens to barter!

She spent days getting our clothes ready. As it happened,
our cousins from Montreal, Ronny and Terry were on one
of their extended visits so she included them too. It was a
cold day when we all piled into the flat-bottomed sleigh and
made the twelve-mile trek into town. Audrey and I sat stiff
as boards under the buffalo robe so that we wouldn't wrinkle
our starched middy dresses, and the boys huddled under
blankets to shut out the cold.

The hotel smelled of cigar smoke and hot gumrubbers,
and a circle of men sat around the lobby on red leather chairs.
A sign with a large arrow pointed up the stairs, and the seven
of us marched across the hardwood floor to the landing. The
boys had taken off their coats and they looked like choir boys
with their white, starched shirts and black ties. Their hair
had been slicked down with vaseline and my ringlets, which
had been tied up in rags all night, bobbed against my back.

The photographer was a very nervous man and, after taking the handful of change my mother handed him and counting it to make sure it added up to two dollars, he lined us up against a black sheet on one wall. It looked like Father wasn't going to part with his pipe, but the man gently eased it out of his mouth as if he was taking a lollipop from a child and, with two fingers, laid it gingerly on a chair. He seated Father and Mother in the centre, placed Audrey and I on either side and told the brothers, since they were the tallest, to line up at the back. Ronny and Terry were to sit Indian-style on the floor in the front — and that's when all the trouble began.

Ronny roared that he wanted to stand at the back with the boys, even though he was a good head shorter. Emerson kept banging his boot against Father's chair in a steady rhythm, which caused Mother to whirl around and slap him somewhere in the midriff. In doing so, she caught the top of my head, and the big, green bow which sat on my crown anchored by one hairpin slid over my eye and completely blocked my vision. Earl had to go to the bathroom. Father got up and retrieved his pipe, muttering that it looked like we were going to be a while and he might as well have a smoke.

The photographer was beginning to perspire as he wrung his hands and tried to decide what to do with this unmanageable family. After what seemed like hours he had us back in order and, by paying Ronny and Terry a nickel each, he was able to talk them into squatting on the floor at our feet. He put his head under the black cover — there was a blinding flash of light — and the whole thing was over.

He ushered us out into the hall so fast we hardly realized we were finished, and promised that the picture, one print only, would be arriving in the mail in a few days. Even though there were other people waiting, the photographer went back into his room and quietly shut the door, mumbling in an exhausted voice that it would be a few minutes before he could work again.

We watched the mailbox for days, waiting anxiously for the results of that day at the photographers. Audrey said she

13

bet we were the only ones on the Northcote road who had a picture taken by a professional. Finally, the big, brown envelope arrived and we gathered around the kitchen table for this important event.

The picture was about a foot square. Mother and Audrey and I looked quite presentable, but the photographer had forgotten to ask Father to relinquish his pipe again and it hung from his mouth like a wooden coathanger. Emerson's tongue was hanging down his chin, a feat he could accomplish with astonishing ease. Earl, who was not allowed enough time in the bathroom, looked to be in pain and Ronny had crossed his eyes. Little cousin Terry, as always, looked like an angel.

Unfortunately, the few of us who were presentable were not enough to make the picture a success. Mother sighed deeply, looked around at the culprits and said, ''Well, there goes two dollars.'' ''Come easy, go easy,'' could be heard from Father behind the *Ottawa Farm Journal*.

RONNY'S BARBERSHOP

A s well as contending with the trials of the depression during the 1930s, our mother carried a workload that would stagger most people today. Even though we children could work alongside any man, there still seemed to be just one more chore Mother had to do before she could sit down to read the *Philadelphia Inquirer* or the *Renfrew Mercury* — or to enjoy that favourite evening pastime, browsing through the Eaton's catalogue. By the time the last one of us had our sponge bath and our cup of cocoa, Mother was usually dog-tired.

So when Ronny, our mischievous Montreal cousin, had an idea that would make our mother's life easier, we leapt at the suggestion.

Ronny noticed how many hours it took Mother to cut our hair since there were seven young heads, counting two visiting cousins. He suggested that, the next time our parents went into town for the weekly supplies, he would tackle the laborious task of cutting all our hair.

We thought it was a wonderful idea, especially when Ronny launched into a theatrical description of our poor mother spending a full evening at the chore, which could be put to better use. So the very next time our parents headed into town on a Saturday, they were scarcely down the lane when Ronny tore into the house and brought all the trappings for the job out on the front lawn to set up.

Everett had a moment of panic and asked if Ronny really knew what he was doing. The novice barber said sure, only that morning he had practiced on a sheep in the enclosure behind the barn. Among Ronny's talents was his uncanny knack of convincing people he knew exactly what he was talking about, when there was little evidence to back him up.

Everett jumped up on the pork barrel we had rolled out of the summer kitchen, and Ronny quickly clamped a flour bag sheet around his neck. Using the comb as a guide, he plunged into the job at hand and we saw great clusters of Everett's golden hair fall to the ground. Ronny started at the back and worked his way to the front; and we watched, horrified, as Everett's head took on the appearance of a stepladder. There were deep ridges of hair and, in some places, we could see his pink scalp peeking through.

Ronny sensed he had a lot to learn. ''We'll make it good and short, then it won't have to be done again for a while,'' he said. He was hacking away like someone possessed and, to avoid being the next victim, Emerson and Earl ran to the barn to hide in the hayloft. But there was no turning back for Everett. Ronny continued his assault on his head while Audrey and I stood transfixed. More and more of Everett's hair fell to the ground, until all that was left was a short uneven stubble. When Ronny was satisfied, he shoved the mirror under Everett's nose, and I was surprised to hear him say he liked it. My sister and I thought he looked terrible, but what Everett couldn't see were the ridges in the back.

Ronny thought I could do with just a trim. Audrey thought I could do without a cut of any description. Over at the barn we could see Emerson and Earl peeking out of the little trap door in the hayloft.

Ronny, even though he was much younger than Audrey, was persuasive, and soon I was sitting up on the pork barrel with the sheet around my neck. I felt him take hold of a cluster of long ringlets at the back of my head and heard the scissors make their cut. Then Audrey's body hit the barrel and Ronny at the same time. He went rolling with the scissors and three long ringlets still clutched in his hand.

When I saw my hair, I cried like a banshee — mostly because I knew the fate that awaited all of us when Mother returned. Audrey cleaned up the mess in the yard, but there was nothing she could do to correct the assault on Everett's and my head.

My brother wore a cap to church for weeks, and had to put up with the growing-in performance as best he could. As for me, Ronny's experiment with scissors was the reason two braids replaced my long, red ringlets for a spell.

*L*ADY OF LISTS

M y mother was an efficiency expert long before the study of time and motion was ever taken seriously in the county. She believed there was an efficient way and an inefficient way to do everything — from setting out the supper dishes to putting on our clothes in the morning — and she constantly made long detailed notes to back up her theories.

This generous use of lists was the bane of our existence when we were youngsters, and we were prone to making jokes about them behind her back. Emerson, who was the comedian of the family, used to say he couldn't go to the privy because Mother hadn't put it on her list.

Every list was constantly under revision in Mother's quest for greater efficiency. Often we came home to find our work lists covered with black crayon marks and switched entries. Audrey would be slated to shovel snow instead of peeling potatoes since she was already outside bringing in wood and it was a waste of steps if she had to come in, change, and then start peeling potatoes. This kind of reasoning had us in a constant state of turmoil. We came to loathe the lists almost as much as we loathed some of the jobs set out on them.

Mother's lists got the best workout when we were expecting company or it was time for fall housecleaning. During those days of great and terrible decision making, she spent hours at the kitchen table preparing her lists so that the chores could be done with the greatest ease and in the most efficient manner possible.

Audrey and I thought it was ridiculous to list such routine things as changing the beds. We all knew that every Monday morning the beds were stripped and nothing interfered with that routine. Nonetheless, every Sunday night Mother would re-arrange the weekly chore lists; inevitably, and to our irritation, the entry to change the beds headed Audrey's and my string of duties.

Father thought the lists were a complete and total waste of time. A man knew what had to be done, and it didn't much matter in what order he did the chores as long as the work was accomplished. Mother insisted he would have much more leisure time if he would allow her to re-organize his workday, but he steadfastly refused to change his work habits. It was the closest we ever saw our parents get to an out-and-out argument.

Like his father and his father before him, our father would go out to the barn in the morning to feed the stock, milk the cows, clean out the manure and strip the separator — all in that order. Father insisted that no list in the world would make things any easier.

Mother said she was going to give it a try despite his stubborn protests. Father took on the look he always wore when he closed his mind to a new and foreign idea, but Mother was not to be discouraged. She followed him through his morning routine for about a week making notes all the while. Father worked around her. After making several adjustments, she finally came up with what she thought was an excellent plan to create a smoother system. Father adamantly insisted there was no need for collecting more idle minutes since he wasn't going anywhere anyhow.

Ignoring that last comment, Mother took out a fresh sheet of foolscap and, with a heavy black crayon, earnestly began to organize Father's routine in the barn. The next morning she took the list to the cow byre and tacked it on the wall right next to the pitchfork. Strategically placed, it would serve as a constant reminder to Father of the exact order in which he was to do the chores. Father gave it nary a glance. Mother had learned that he often came around to her way of thinking eventually, so she did nothing more than slap the list with satisfaction when it had been tacked up and nod in his direction.

We children had already gotten out the milk stools and were heading for the cows when Mother left the barn to put breakfast on the table. Father always wore a hat and, in the summertime, it was a wide tattered straw. In the winter, it was a fur-lined navy melton cloth apparition with ear lugs tied under his chin. That day he had on the navy melton. Mother was no sooner out of the barn when he undid the ties from under his chin and walked over to the list. He found a nail at the top of the foolscap and, with more force than was necessary, slammed the hat over the list completely obliterating it from view.

Every morning thereafter he did exactly the same thing. He'd walk out into the barn, take off the hat, slap it over the list and get down to business. The list was never mentioned again. For all I know Mother may have thought he was following it to the letter. Certainly none of us kids had the courage to tell her exactly what Father thought of her exercise in efficiency.

GRANNY HINES

Granny Hines was a most formidable old lady who lived on the farm next to us. She was just a wisp of a thing, in a long black dress with many white pinnies on top of each other, and a cloud of white hair that swirled around her face like candy floss. She had more impact on our lives than we liked to admit, and everyone in the community called her Granny, even though she was only related to those who lived in the small black log house with her.

Her five granddaughters played with us and took the long walk with us to school, and we were in almost constant contact with the family. This was a mixed blessing because, if it weren't for Granny Hines, I probably would not have grown up terrified of the dark, convinced that ghosts walked the fields of our farm at night. Or that the dead were just waiting to come back to haunt us and that we should never touch a casket at a wake. Or that daily prayers, although necessary, carried with them certain taboos which we had to observe or we would be in dire trouble.

Even though many years have passed since Granny Hines influenced our lives, I still find myself pausing when, in the middle of a silent prayer, I commit one of the cardinal sins she warned us against back then.

Granny said it was quite all right to pray at our mother's knee, which was a good thing because Mother would tolerate nothing else. But the old woman said we should silently continue our prayers when we got into bed too. She said God

21

would have a difficult time separating one child's prayers from another unless we made separate appeals. This all sounded perfectly logical to me. But there were some things, she warned, we had to be especially careful about. I found myself mentally checking off all the things that would anger God, or cause him to ignore what were very specific and special prayers silently offered in the confines of the big feather tickings when the lamp was blown out.

For instance, Granny said if you yawned in the middle of a prayer you had to start all over again. She gave no explanation, but said we just had to trust her — the prayer was useless if we let out even a hint of a yawn. Needless to say, just knowing I couldn't yawn invariably caused me to yawn uncontrollably. I would fall asleep thinking that God had given up on me in disgust and moved on to listen to someone else's worthier prayers. Even though I now realize it doesn't matter a whit to God if I yawn or not, I find myself scanning the congregation in the midst of the benediction to determine which of the members is about to have his prayers erased with a simple yawn.

She also said it was plain useless to pray if your hands weren't in steeples. She vowed she knew many a person who was struck dead because she prayed while she was busy at washing dishes, or driving the car, and because she didn't care enough to stop and put her hands in order. When we asked for names, she cleverly avoided the issue, but assured us there were many in the cemetary that would have said their prayers with their hands in the steeple position if they had it to do over again.

And we might as well have prayed to the devil as prayed to God with our mouths full of chewing gum. According to Granny Hines, God hated chewing gum. So we were especially careful, if we happened to have a wad in our mouths, to plant it someplace where we could get it back after prayers.

Granny Hines said, too, that we all took too much for granted with our prayers. Once we left our mother's knee and continued our silent prayers in bed, God had no way of knowing who He was talking to, so we had to identify ourselves. She said the best thing to do was to say, "It's Mary down here in Renfrew County," so all of my silent prayers were prefaced by this bit of added information for God's ears. I grew up convinced that my prayers would be in vain unless God knew exactly who was talking to him, so often as an added precaution I would tack on, "You know, God, Mary with the red hair and freckles."

Granny's list of do's and don'ts in praying was longer than the Beatitudes, and we were hard-pressed to remember all of them. I often wonder now how we were taken in by her outlandish stories. But back then, Granny Hines was our entertainment. She was a moving picture show, books we couldn't afford and trips to another land.

We hated and loved everything she was at the same time. We shivered over her ghost stories, and her tales about death and destruction and how we could fall into God's disfavour. But when it came time to sit around the old rocking chair in the parlour and listen to her tales, there wasn't one of us who didn't want to be there.

THE SALVATION ARMY BAND

M other wanted her children to be completely consumed by the spirit of Christmas, and took advantage of every opportunity to involve us in any activity that would emphasize what was, to her, the most important of all holiday celebrations. So it was that on a bitterly cold December Saturday night the five of us were bundled into our warmest winter clothing, wrapped in heavy quilts, piled into the two-seater cutter and driven into town to sing on the street corner with the Salvation Army band. It did not matter to Mother that we were strong supporters of the Lutheran faith. The Salvation Army offered us another opportunity to absorb more of the season's spirit and that was what really counted.

We were a singing family. Intermittently we sang in the church choir and at concerts with our mother accompanying us on the harmonica. We spent hours daily with our voices raised in song and, later on, we got an old pump organ in a trade. Singing was a marvellous form of family entertainment when I was growing up — the most appealing aspect of it was that it was free.

I loved the look of the Salvation Army band, especially in the winter. They were wonderful to see — the women in their long navy capes, their bonnets trimmed with scarlet, and the men with their snappy hats and heavy reefer coats sporting shiny brass buttons. I often asked my mother why we couldn't join the Army. As far as I was concerned, no one in our church looked as smart and I was sure I would have no trouble mastering the tambourine.

By the time we reached the street corner the band had chosen, they were well into their service. Only a few people who were not of their faith had joined them but that didn't matter to us. We piled out of the cutter — that is to say, we children and our mother. Father elected to spend the evening at Thacker's garage. He thought the whole idea was crazy and said that anyone who stood out on a street corner in the dead of winter blowing on a tuba and shaking a tin plate couldn't be 100 percent. As usual Mother paid him no heed, but boldly pushed us into their circle. Then she fell right into the spirit of things by taking out her harmonica and playing all the old, best-loved Christmas carols in harmony.

I can remember we weren't the least bit shy about the whole experience. Many of the townspeople passed us and gave us odd stares. I suppose we must have presented quite a picture — the Salvation Army band in all its regalia and we country children, wrapped up like mummies, led by a tall, stately matron playing harmony on a harmonica. But back then we had few inhibitions — if our mother said we were to sing on a street corner on a freezing winter's night, then that was what we would merrily do.

Stamping our feet to keep warm, we felt our mouths grow stiff from the cold, but we were having the time of our lives. I felt so filled with the Christmas spirit that I imagined I could reach out and touch it.

Then a young woman in the band came over and asked me if I would like to try the tambourine. I was so thrilled that I never once gave a thought to the possibility that I couldn't play it. I had scarcely taken my eyes off the woman all night. I had watched her give it a twist and a shake, then hit it against the heel of her hand; occasionally she would lower it and slap it against her leg. When I began to shake it, I knew I was out of rhythm but that certainly didn't concern me. For good measure, I even threw in a few slaps against my snowsuit-covered hip.

Then the man, who was clearly the head of the whole group, asked me what song I would like the choir to sing next. The only song that came to mind was *Bringing in the Sheaves*. It certainly wasn't a Christmas carol, but that didn't seem to matter and soon we were belting it out with great gusto.

Perhaps due to the freezing temperatures, or maybe because the band had exhausted its repertoire, the concert came to an abrupt end. We were invited into the hall for refreshments, which was much more than we had bargained for. With quick enthusiasm we accepted, and soon our hands were cupping steaming mugs of hot chocolate as we munched on homemade cookies. Running through my mind was the possibility that we might be joining the Salvation Army after all since we were being made to feel so welcome. Then I overheard my mother telling the Major that we were Lutherans. By her tone of voice, there was no room for doubt that she had any intention of changing. Nonetheless, the evening was a marvellous experience for us all.

All the way home, Father lamented that everyone in Thacker's garage was joking about our joining the Salvation Army. But nothing could break the spell of that wonderful night. Each of us felt enveloped in the true spirit of Christmas as Mother had hoped we would.

$\mathcal{A}$ WINTER DRIVE IN THE MODEL T

I t seems to me now, so many years later, that our winters were more severe than they are today. I remember fences completely covered over with drifts, and bitterly cold nights when the roof would crackle from the frost and the water in the wash basin would be frozen solid when we rose in the morning.

We tried to be prepared for the unexpected during those harsh winters of the 1930s — Mother and Father always expected the winter to be hard and long. Every year, just after the first snow arrived, my father would drive the old Model T into the car shed, raise it up on four blocks, remove the wheels, put heavy quilts over its hood and bed it down until spring. That is, until one winter when Mother persuaded him to leave the car out so we could take a run into town when the spirit moved us.

"Folks don't stash the car away anymore Albert, they leave it out. After all, we don't live at the North Pole." My father tried to tell her that to take the old Model T anywhere in a Renfrew County winter was courting disaster, but we all knew Father had lost the battle before it even began.

Mother also thought that winding down the old year without a bit of excitement was like admitting to the world that you had lost your spirit of adventure. So it was that, between Christmas and New Year's that year, in spite of the loudest protests from Father, we were all herded into the car to take a drive into town to look at the store windows. Four of us piled into the back, with the other one wedged between Mother and Father in the front seat. Hot bricks were wrapped in newspaper, then in grain bags, and placed at our feet. Big quilts circled our bodies tying us into a common bundle, and Father went around the car to make sure the side curtains were well fastened down. The car coughed a few times in protest but, after Father's persistant cranking, it was soon purring like a barn cat.

It was touch and go navigating the long lane, but Father followed the path made by the big sleigh and we reached the road without mishap. The wind was howling fiercely, and the side curtains were scant protection, but we were all so excited about going into town to look in the store windows that no one complained.

Briscoe's store was just ahead. We could see the light about a mile down the road. Father was storming in the front seat that not another soul would venture out on a night like this, and that only fools would tamper with disaster by making the twelve-mile trip into town by car when the drifts had all but eliminated any sense of direction.

Then we were at the store, and Father swung the car up to the steps and said he would slip in for some pipe tobacco in case it was closed on our way home. He climbed out over the door, because he knew the car door had been known to freeze on a bitterly cold night. On more than one occasion, he had driven hanging on to the thing to keep it closed. We could see a few heads inside the store, but there wasn't a car or horse in sight. It looked like some of the Briscoe's neighbours had walked there for their weekly confab.

Father came out and the frost swirled over his head as he breathed in the freezing night air. He reached in and grabbed the crank and went to the front of the car. It kicked a few times, but otherwise showed no sign of life. Mother reached under the wheel and worked the throttle, and Father continued to crank. It was soon obvious to us all that there wasn't an ounce of life in the old car.

Emerson figured it was just a matter of time until our bodies would be frozen, and there was a good chance we would be beyond reviving by the time anyone discovered us. I started to cry and Mother gave me a swat that increased my panic. "Don't be silly, Emerson, there are plenty of men in the store and we can go in there if your father can't get the car going. Now hush up all of you." Father would stop every few minutes to light his pipe and the momentary flame showed us that he was seething.

Finally, there was nothing to do but go back into the store and ask for help. Mr. Briscoe hitched up his team of horses, positioned them in front of the car, and hitched a chain to the undercarriage. In minutes, we were being hauled home by the only sensible means of transportation there was for county roads in December, according to our father.

By mid-morning the next day, there was the old Model T up on its winter blocks in the drive shed with a few old blankets thrown over its hood. The only comment we ever heard about the whole episode was when Father said at the supper table, "Yes sir, the only way to treat these Renfrew County winters is with the utmost respect."

THE GRAB BAG

I t was only the second time I had ever had twenty-five cents of my own. The first time, at the height of my ecstasy, I had to part with the quarter so that Mother could buy coal oil for the lamps. It was a tragedy when it happened, but disappointments during the depression came as regularly as measles and winter 'flu.

But this time the money was mine to keep. Mother promised me that I could do with it as I wished. The twenty-five-cent reward came from the Renfrew County board of education — I had earned it for good penmanship — and I knew just how I was going to spend it.

I had been eyeing the big woven basket in front of Ritza's drugstore in Renfrew for weeks. Every Saturday when we took our weekly trip into town for our supplies, I would run up the street to the drugstore, as fast as my legs could carry me, to make sure the basket was still there. The sign said "Grab Bags — twenty-five cents," and underneath another sign said "Satisfaction guaranteed, or money cheerfully refunded."

I couldn't imagine anyone not being satisfied. Certainly, everyone I saw who picked up one of the little brown paper bags with the twisted top held securely by string wore happy smiles on their faces. I tried to imagine what would be inside. Perhaps an expensive bottle of perfume? Or maybe a piece of fine jewelry — a ring — how I longed for a ring with a big glass stone.

I told my mother what I planned to do with my award money. I knew she would have been happier had I spent a nickel of it and put the rest away, but she had promised I could spend it as I wished. I thought Saturday would never come and, when it did, I worked like a beaver helping with the chores so that we would get an early start. The quarter was tied with a tight knot in the corner of my best handkerchief, and I tied and untied it all the way into town.

The car was parked at Thacker's garage, and I jumped clear of the running board and was half way to Ritza's drugstore by the time Mother hollered, "Be back here in ten minutes." I was gasping for breath by the time I reached the store, but there stood the wicker basket filled to the brim with the little twisted brown paper bags.

The druggist came up to me. "Can I feel them?" I asked. He assured me I could and then added, "Do you intend to buy one?" I thrust the knotted hanky in his direction to confirm that I was there to do business.

I poked my hand down to the bottom of the basket. Some bags felt soft, as if they held cotton batten. I had already made up my mind if I could not feel a ring through the bag, I would settle for a bottle of expensive perfume. There didn't seem to be any jewelry, but one bag definitely held a bottle. I was sure it would be something exquisite like *Lily of the Valley*. I held the bag in my hand for a few minutes trying to decide — and what a decision it was. After all, I was about to spend a fortune and I wanted to be sure of my investment.

The druggist was shuffling from one foot to the other as I untied my hanky and handed him the money. Then I tore out of the store with my grab bag and didn't stop running until I hit Thacker's garage.

To prolong the delight, I decided to open the bag on the way home in the car. Mother looked at it with some doubt. "So you spent your money and you don't even know what you bought." I assured her it was perfume, and probably very expensive too.

The car was out of town when I allowed myself the pleasure of untying the string. Inside I saw a bright pink label; I was sure it was some delicate brand I had never heard of before. I took out the bottle and there was the same lady's face staring at me that looked down from the medicine shelf over the kitchen sink. In an arc in bold, black print were the words "Lydia Pinkham's Elixir for Pale People."

I thought I was going to be sick. I begged Mother to stop the car and turn back so I could get a refund, but she wouldn't hear of it. She said I had made a deal and, as far as she was concerned, the matter was closed. I thought of my money and knew it would be a long time before I had that much again.

I was so angry, I shoved the bottle of medicine back in the bag and threw it on the floor of the car. When we drove into the yard I grabbed it and jumped off the runningboard, heading for the watering trough. I took a whiff just to make sure someone hadn't made a mistake and that, by some miracle, it was *Lily of the Valley* trapped inside a Lydia Pinkham's bottle, but there was no mistaking that smell. I watched it dribble into the water, and got absolutely no satisfaction from the thought that the magic preventative medicine would put a rose in the cheeks of the cows, or a prance in the feet of the horses when they drank it.

AUNTIE'S WINTER VISITS

With the coming of winter on the farm also came a maiden aunt. As soon as the first snap of frost hit the air, we could expect a letter to arrive in the mail to inform us that she would be arriving in a few days to spend the winter months with us.

At the time I thought she was very elderly. She stooped slightly when she walked and the hair on top of her head was like white down, but she had the clearest blue eyes I had ever seen. As my mother would say, "Don't try to put anything over on her because she's as sharp as a tack."

Many of the farm neighbours in our community also had maiden aunts come for the winter months, and it was much later that I learned that these relatives in transit came because they had nowhere else to go. There were no nursing homes in our area then, and only the destitute went to the county home. Families accepted the responsibility of caring for their aged relatives, and we came to accept having Auntie around each winter as readily as we accepted having grandparents and cousins for long spells during the summer.

Auntie would arrive with her tapestry tote bag bulging with all her earthly possessions. Unlike other relatives who came to visit, we knew there would be no treats for the children because Auntie had no money. Nonetheless, we looked forward to her visits because she had a marvellous sense of humour and told wonderful German fairy tales that kept us entertained for hours. We learned poems and recitations and, if her *rhumatiz* — as she called it — wasn't bothering her too much, she would dance a kind of jig while our mother played the Sailor's Hornpipe on the harmonica.

But Auntie wasn't only there for frivolity. She had a fierce sense of pride and wanted very much to earn her keep, so it was her task every winter to get us caught up with the mending. I suspect now that our mother deliberately saved the socks with holes for weeks so that she would have something to keep Auntie busy. But I remember how enthralled I was with the way she mended them. She brought her own little sewing kit with her, and in it was a black wooden darner which she would thrust into the toes of the stockings. When she had stretched the hole out tight, she would circle it with long stitches, and then weave the darning wool back and forth over the hole; when she finished, we could scarcely tell where the mended spot was.

She wore a large, white pinny over a plain, black dress, and kept many straight pins on the bib of the apron at the ready for any sewing job at hand. For the first few days of her visit the apron was taken upstairs with her at night, but when she started to feel more at home she would take it off at bedtime and hang it with the other aprons on the coat hook at the back door, just like a member of the family.

She wasn't above disciplining us either. Just because she was visiting didn't mean she felt like an outsider! When our mother would reprimand us, we could always count on Auntie throwing in "Now you young 'uns mind your ma, ya hear?" It would never occur to us to have anything but the utmost respect for the old lady, so we took the discipline as we would from our parents. They thought it was good for us to have the elderly around; it taught us tolerance, my father would say.

Auntie would stay on most of the winter, sometimes leaving to go to another relative for Christmas, and coming back in January until the snow melted. Then, when the time came, she would get ready to move on to another household.

"It's time to get over to Elmer's and Sadie's, they'll be looking for me. I like to be there by the time the sap is runnin','' she'd say. One morning we'd take her letter to Briscoe's store to mail on our way to school, and we knew it would be a letter saying her visit with us was coming to an end and she was ready for yet another move.

$\mathcal{M}$Y BANKING CAREER

T he whole idea to Father was just a shade off centre. He had never heard of children being encouraged to put money in the bank, and as far as he was concerned the teacher had gone too far this time. Besides didn't anyone know there was a depression going on. . .where were these pennies to come from?

The issue was the penny bank deposits, a system wherein each pupil was asked to bring money to school in the hope of encouraging thrift and promoting a desire to save. Of course the teacher had not counted on the dour, cautious people in the area who, like my father, grew up believing that money put in the bank was gone forever.

I can remember coming home from school that first day in September with my three brothers and sisters, each of us clutching a little oblong box. Printed on the side was "a penny saved is a penny earned." The boxes were to be returned to school the next day after our parents had seen them and confirmed that Miss Crosby was not collecting the money for her own use.

That first day Miss Crosby went to great lengths to explain the penny bank deposit boxes to us. We would put coins in as often as we could, keeping track in individual record books, and once a week the boxes would be emptied and the money taken into Renfrew to be deposited into something called a bank account which would be in our own name.

We were very excited when we burst into the house that night to explain this wonderful news to our parents. We were sure in a matter of time we would all be millionaires. But as soon as we mentioned the word "bank" the trouble began.

Father immediately put a damper on the whole idea. As far as he was concerned the bank was just about the most unsafe place in the county to put your money. "It's all mixed up in there with everybody elses, and besides, who is to say the bank won't go broke too. And then where would you be with your penny deposit boxes?" His voice was getting louder, and he kept throwing in a German word here and there which we all knew were cuss words he didn't have the nerve to say in English.

Mother kept saying, "Now Albert, I'm sure the banks are honest and Miss Crosby wouldn't get the children involved in an off-centre scheme." "Horsefeathers," Father roared.

We all fondled our penny deposit boxes that were causing the trouble. Finally, Mother ended the argument by saying, "We'll let them try it. After all, they aren't going to have much to put in them anyway, and they can't be the only pupils in the school not taking part." We tossed Father the most baleful looks we could muster. He buried his head in the *Ottawa Farm Journal*, and blue clouds of smoke rising from his pipe were evidence enough that he wasn't convinced but that the argument was over.

We took the boxes back to school the next day — each with a penny inside that Mother had taken from the bowl in the cupboard — and our boxes joined the others on the front windowsill opposite Miss Crosby's desk. As often as we could, we trucked up to the windowsill during the week and dropped a few more pennies inside, making suitable entries in the record book under Miss Crosby's watchful eye.

Then Friday rolled around and, just before the day ended, the teacher gathered up the boxes, opened the flaps on the bottom and, to our horror, mixed the entire contents of twenty-seven deposit boxes together on the top of her desk. Emerson was the first to hiss out "I knew it, Father was right. We'll never see our money again, it's all just one big blob.

Nobody is going to ever figure that mess out.'' Miss Crosby glared down, and he shut up like a steel trap. She did some fast calculations and dumped our entire fortunes into a brown sack; we just knew it was gone forever.

We went home dragging our feet, wondering how we were going to break the news to our parents. Unless some genius could straighten out the mess, no one would know who had how much. Father was jubilant, delighted that he was proven right. But Mother still insisted that the right amount would find its way into the right account. For the first time, we doubted she was as wise as we had believed.

On Monday, the penny deposit boxes were back on the windowsill, and on each desk were little books with our names on them. We gingerly opened them, and were astonished to find the amount tallied with that in our record books. Perhaps all was not lost after all. We brought a few pennies again that week, figuring we'd give the system a bit longer.

We still couldn't figure how we could get the money out if we wanted it, but Miss Crosby assured us we could. That test came when months later we all wrote a cheque to the Red Cross for ten cents each and, sure enough, a week later our bank book showed that we had taken out ten cents.

I don't suppose each of us ever had more than a dollar in the bank all the time we lived on the farm, but the penny deposit boxes were enough to convince us that indeed a penny saved was a penny earned. However, Father never did trust the banks. Whatever money he had, he continued to keep in the glass bowl in the kitchen cupboard with his gold watch and his ivory-handled jack knife.

FATHER AND THE EYE MAN

Something had to be done. That's all there was to it. Mother noticed the problem when she saw that Father was beginning to hold the *Renfrew Mercury* farther and farther away from his eyes. There were other signs that he was having difficulty focusing. He could no longer tell the time on the gingerbread clock in the kitchen unless he stood across the room; and once he called Earl "Everett." Although I strongly suspect he simply had his mind on something else, Mother used the incident as another piece of ammunition to insist that Father go to see the Eye Man, as he was called then.

The next Saturday, when we were in town getting the week's supplies, Father found himself in the doctor's office for an examination. We tagged along to see the performance, and were left in the sparsely furnished waiting room with strict orders to behave. There was no need for a warning; we were always so awed by the atmosphere in the office of any professional that we scarcely breathed.

After what seemed like a very long time, we heard Father in heated debate with Mother and the doctor. His voice carried right through the tongue-and-groove partition of the office. There was obviously something very much awry. Then he was out the door with Mother in hot pursuit and the bewildered doctor trailing behind.

When we saw that Father wasn't even going to stop long enough to acknowledge his children, we slid off the bench and followed our parents outside where the debate con-

39

tinued. Father, we surmised through the bits and pieces of half-English half-German dialogue, was outraged over the two-dollar examination fee. To add insult to injury, the doctor expected another three dollars when the glasses were ready. He ranted that you could buy a good heifer for five dollars, and there was absolutely no way he was going to be taken in by the likes of that bandit.

A small group of bystanders collected on the street, and one man who seemed a bit worse for wear yelled, "Give it to 'im, Albert." Mother glared at the man as though he were just a slip less than human. She was fast losing patience with Father as well, but any attempt to reason with him fell on deaf ears. He had been taken, plain and simple. Even the suggestion that he would soon have to have one of us read the weekly paper to him failed to change his mind. He could do nothing about the two dollars he had already spent, but he absolutely refused to pad the pockets of that man any further.

He headed for the five-and-dime store, and went straight to the eye glass counter where there were dozens of pairs of glasses laid out in neat rows. On a stand was a piece of printed cardboard with various sizes of lettering on it. Father started at one end of the row and tried pair after pair, testing them on the chart until he found a pair he could read with.

Mother insisted he would be severely damaging his eyes, but he had his sights on the seventy-five-cent price tag and there was no changing his mind. "These are just fine," he insisted, standing in the aisle of the store looking clear through to the back. "That sign back on the wall says 'oilcloth twenty-five cents a yard' and if I can see that far, I'll sure be able to see the paper."

"They're window glass, just plain window glass," Mother countered. Father had picked up a package off the counter and was reading fast and furious, something he hadn't been able to do for a long time. "I tell you woman, they are just fine and besides, I even get a free glasses case. That's more than I'd of got from that highway robber down the street."

He was starting to work himself into another lather. Mother, sensing she had lost the war, started walking out of the store with all of us in tow.

Father paid for the glasses, tucking them into the blue hard case that snapped shut with a hollow clap and putting them in his overall pocket.

The issue was closed; but as we all headed for the car, we knew it would be a very silent trip home. Mother sure hated to lose an argument.

Father wore the glasses for years, and when one of the legs fell off, he wired it back on with rabbit snare. During the day they sat on the clock shelf in the kitchen, but they were the first thing he headed for when he came in at night after the chores were done. They had silver frames and little round lenses and, according to Father, it was the best seventy-five cents he had ever spent.

He never forgot the two dollars he paid out to the Eye Man for nothing. For years after, every time Mother was about to enter into a financial deal of any description, Father would relate the story of the time she talked him into the eye examination. We would hear how he was relieved of two dollars and had absolutely nothing to show for it, and we'd all learn once again how a fool and his money were soon parted.

AUDREY'S HIGH-HEELED SHOES

D uring the depression my mother could account for every penny that came in or went out of the house. But although we constantly got lectures on the hardships of the 1930s, it was amazing how Mother could find a bit of extra cash for what she considered essentials.

Her theory was that there were some things children should not be deprived of just because there was a depression, and it was her job to find a way of providing those few amenities that separated us from the poor folks. That is not to say we weren't poor — we were — but Mother, with her New York City background, felt the reality was easier to face if it could be softened occasionally by a bit of frivolity. So it came to pass that Audrey, while every other teenage girl at school was wearing heavy, brown, laced-up brogues, was to have a pair of high-heeled pumps.

Father thought Mother had taken leave of her senses. When the binder needed a new belt, the Model T could use a new spare tire and he couldn't recall the last time the saws had been professionally sharpened, how could she be thinking of high-heeled shoes? But Mother stuck to her guns. Audrey was tall for her age, she was obedient, she was mature beyond her years and besides, she was a child who never asked for a thing. Father thought all of those reasons were inconsequential, but Mother had made up her mind and it wasn't a decision that could be easily reversed.

Now, so rare an occasion was the buying of a new pair of high-heeled shoes that, when the day finally rolled around that Mother had enough nickels and dimes in the blue jug on the back-to-the-wall cupboard to make the big purchase, the entire family — with the exception of Father — headed into Renfrew for the transaction. Father claimed to the bitter end that Mother had taken leave of her senses and anyone who would throw away $2.95 on a pair of high-heeled shoes for a girl who was barely into her teens needed to have her head examined.

As often happened when Father was left behind on the farm to chew on his pipe, we five children, with Mother at the wheel of the car, sang all the way into town. It was a marvellous early summer day and, as if to herald Mother's decision, trilliums and wild violets were sprouting all along the roadway, adding to our feeling of gaiety.

We all trouped into Scott's shoe store as if it was a common occurrence to go in on a Saturday and ask for a pair of high-heeled shoes. Audrey had worn a pair of Mother's fine lisle stockings for the day, and Mr. Scott went to great pains to make sure of her foot size by asking her to stand on the big steel ruler. He went into the back of the store and brought out several boxes, and when he opened them, we all started to talk at once.

Audrey liked the patent ones, I liked the ones with a bit of red leather at the toes and the boys liked the ones with big flappy tongues. We discounted those at once, because they reminded us too much of the old brogues we had worn into town. Mother made sure Mr. Scott realized she was not prepared to spend a penny over $2.95, and she sat with her purse clutched tightly in her hands signifying that was where the princely sum was stored.

Audrey decided she liked the patent ones best. The heels were about two inches high, and she was most reluctant to walk on the rug in the store where everyone making a purchase tried out the new shoes. She was suddenly attacked by a wave of shyness, but Mother said if she didn't get up and walk immediately, Mr. Scott could put the shoes back in the box and we'd leave.

Audrey hobbled over to the rug and took a walk to the end of the store. She moved like she was passing over a log bridge; but by the time she had been up and down the rug twice, she had mastered the art of walking in the high heels and looked like she was born with them on her feet.

Mr. Scott said the shoes were worth far more than $2.95, but a special purchase had allowed him to offer them to his best customers for that low price. Mother reminded him we hadn't bought shoes in his store for a donkey's age, and therefore shouldn't be considered best customers. In any case, she doubted the shoes were worth a cent more than the price she read on the end of the box. Audrey was already out of the store with the shoes on her feet, so Mother opened her purse on the counter, turned it upside down and paid for the shoes in nickels and dimes.

Mother allowed her to wear the new shoes as far as Thacker's garage, where the car was parked, and then they were put back in the box. Of course, she wasn't to wear them to school — only on special occasions like church — but after Audrey had her first pair of high heels, we all agreed she had changed. She no longer played tag with us after our chores were done, she tried to boss us around a bit more than we liked and, without being asked every Saturday night, she rolled her hair up in rags for church on Sunday morning.

Father didn't like the change at all. He kept reminding Mother that Audrey was simply too young to handle the trauma of high heels as he knew she would be. There was a time and a place for everything and Audrey's time for high heels, he was sure, had come too soon.

MOTHER AND THE
TEMPERANCE MOVEMENT

One of our neighbours who lived far enough away so as not to interfere with our everyday lives was, nonetheless, a force to be reckoned with. My father said she was so religious, she wouldn't say "heck" if she fell into a feeding trough of soft mash, and my mother tried to keep her distance. But, as was the case in smaller rural communities in the 1930s, neighbours came in contact with each other through church affairs, trips to the general store and at wakes and weddings. So, keeping our distance from our holier-than-thou neighbour was not always possible.

She was one of the leading forces behind the movement to keep the town dry. As long as we lived in Renfrew County, liquor had never been sold in the hotel — and as far as this neighbour was concerned, it never would be. She worked diligently to this end, using any platform she could find to promote her cause. She recruited anyone who showed the least leaning toward her thinking and, for reasons which escape me to this day, she thought my mother would be a perfect candidate for her group of abstainers.

It was on one of my mother's trips to Briscoe's store that the woman accosted her and mentioned that a speaker was going to be in attendance at the next temperance meeting and she would be delighted if Mother would go with her. Whether it was because Mother could not think of a reason not to, or if she was just thrilled to have a night off without five children underfoot, I don't know, but she came home and announced that she would be attending the temperance meeting the next night at the Renfrew Hotel.

Father looked at her in utter amazement, as if he'd never laid eyes on her before. Mother had never shown the least inclination to temperance and her sudden interest in the "dry" movement was more than he could comprehend. Besides, she often took a swig of grape wine when we had company, and would wash out vinegar and ketchup bottles whenever it came time for Father to bottle down his home-brew.

When she announced who she was going to the meeting with, my father got that knowing look on his face that showed the whole picture was falling into place. "So the old codger has you brainwashed too, eh?"

Mother protested in the loudest fashion that she was just curious and, besides, she could see the benefits of such a group. After all, she said, liquor had ruined more than one happy home. Emerson threw in the comment that Father sure liked his home-brew and home-made whiskey, and our home certainly wasn't ruined. That contribution sent him to bed early.

The pious neighbour picked up our mother the next night in her shiny late-model car and, although we five children crowded into the doorway to wave our goodbyes, Father never budged from the rocking chair. Mumbling something about it being the silliest thing he ever heard of, he let out a string of phrases in German that we knew were swear words, because the only time he spoke German was when he wanted to say words that were forbidden in our household. When he finally got back to speaking English, it was to tell us that the neighbour was an old busybody who would be better occupied if she paid some attention to her own back yard and left matters alone which shouldn't concern her.

"Did you ever notice how close her eyes are together?" he asked no one in particular. "Never trust anyone who has little beady eyes, I always say." When we five children climbed the stairs to bed, Father was still lamenting in the kitchen.

It wasn't long after that we heard the car swing into the yard. Father chuckled in the kitchen, and we distinctly heard the comment, "Well, I wonder if they're sober." The walls in the old log house were paper thin, and we heard the clinking of glass as Father rushed around the kitchen. We knew he always had a wee nip at night just before he stoked the fire, and we assumed he was rushing around to hide the evidence just in case Mother brought the old busybody in for a cup of tea.

The door swung wide, and Father greeted the two as if his tirade a few hours before had never happened. "Nice night. . . come in. . . how was the meetin'?" When they got settled around the pine table in the kitchen, we heard the familiar squeak of the cupboard.

"Say, I couldn't interest you in a little drink, could I? Best liquor in Renfrew County. . .made it myself. Sure beats green tea on a night like this." We kids were all gathered around the stove pipe in the upstairs hall trying to catch a glimpse of the goings on down in the kitchen. We saw the neighbour fling herself out of the chair and grab her coat and purse. Emerson said she made it to the door in two strides.

We figured Father was really in for it. For the longest time there wasn't a sound coming out of the kitchen, then Mother said she didn't think much of the meeting. They sounded like a lot of busybodies to her; and besides, Renfrew didn't care much what went on in Northcote so, when you got right down to it, why should she mind what was going on in Renfrew. There was another silence and then we heard her say, "Albert, just get me one of those little juice glasses out of the cupboard will you. I'll just have a few drops of that grape wine to take the chill out of my bones."

$\mathcal{E}$NOUGH PANCAKES TO
FEED THE COUNTY

F ather was considered the expert cook for certain dishes. Even though Mother occasionally tried her hand at things like potato pancakes, fried sauerkraut and back bacon, it never really tasted the same. Father always said Mother's French background interfered with her appreciation of German food, and it was just taken for granted that when we had a German dish Father would put it together.

However, one Saturday after our parents left for town to get the week's supplies, Emerson declared that there was no special knack to making potato pancakes. He decided we would surprise them by having supper on the table when they drove into the yard. None of us knew the first thing about how to start, but whenever anyone showed the least hesitation, Emerson immediately set himself up as an authority. It wasn't long before he was firing orders around the kitchen like a five-star general.

Earl and I were ordered to peel the potatoes, and lots of them, because Emerson was sure these were going to be the best pancakes that ever came off the old Findlay oval. Everett was told to grate the potatoes into Mother's big baking bowl while Emerson did little more than set the iron fry pan on the stove. He slapped in several wooden spoonfuls of bacon drippings and before long it was sizzling and giving off small whiffs of blue smoke. He ordered Everett to hurry up with the grating, and we looked with dismay at the mounting heap of darkening potatoes which were accumulating in the bowl. Emerson assured us they would whiten up when he added the eggs.

Audrey was sent to the cellar for a few onions from the sand bins; then she had to peel them, cutting them into huge chunks to toss into the potato mixture. Everett had peeled about a dozen good-sized potatoes and Emerson matched them with an equal number of eggs. We protested and told him we were sure Father only added one or two at the most. Emerson paid no attention to our protests and continued to break one egg after another into the bowl of potatoes, which were now an unsightly dark grey colour.

Then he took the big soup ladle which hung on a nail by the stove and, with a flourish, dumped heaping mounds of the soupy mixture into the sizzling pan. It spread to the full area of the pan like water. We told Emerson that Father's stayed in nice, neat little round shapes; he just sent us withering looks of disgust. We all stood around the stove and watched the smoke rise like a forest fire from the pan.

As he used a knife to peek under the mass, we caught a glimpse of a black crusty bottom. ''Stand back, because I'm going to have to flip it,'' he said. He took the pancake turner and deftly flipped the contents in the air. Miraculously it landed in the pan. When he thought it was cooked, he removed it to a platter and started the whole process over again. The rest of us looked in dismay at the pancake which was about fourteen inches in diameter and black as your boot, but we held our tongues.

Although the pan was full again, Emerson had hardly made a dint in the supply of potatoes and eggs which was getting blacker by the minute. He stood at the stove for a good hour before he finally scooped out the last of the mixture, by which time he had filled a second platter and a large dinner plate. We could have fed most of the county. Nonetheless, Emerson was beside himself with pride. He kept running to the window to see if Mother and Father were coming in the lane.

When they finally walked in the kitchen door, the table was set for supper, with two platters and a dinner plate heaped with black potato pancakes spread along the top like soldiers. Father walked over and took a look at what was before him. He said nothing and Mother went about pouring out a jug of maple syrup and clucking over Emerson's accomplishment.

I made the mistake of saying the pancakes tasted more like omelettes — and burnt ones at that. Emerson went into a rage and accused me of just being plain jealous of what he had produced. Our eyes were on Father. He carefully lifted one of the pancakes off the platter nearest him. It completely covered his plate. After sitting for a few minutes looking at the thing, he took a bite. He chewed for a long time. We followed suit, drenching the pancakes with syrup and butter, but nothing could disguise the burnt taste. As for Emerson, he was diving into his second serving like a man possessed, proclaiming all the time that they were the best pancakes he had ever tasted.

It was soon obvious that we weren't going to polish off the plates full of the remaining pancakes. Mother assured Emerson that we would wrap them and put them in the back shed to freeze for another meal. The rest of us rolled our eyes to the ceiling as thoughts of having to endure another meal of the dreadful pancakes raced through our heads. Huge packets were put out on the pork barrel and, although no one knew what happened to them, gradually the piles got smaller and finally vanished without a trace. Now I think they were worked in with the pigs' feedings — their stomachs being far less fussy than ours were.

$\mathcal{T}$HE ONION LADY

As a large family growing up during the depression, we were a surprisingly healthy lot. We ate good nourishing food, and each winter Mother stirred a daily tablespoon of cod liver oil into our morning porridge. Unlike the oils and vitamins of today, we vowed we could taste the fins in every spoonful we swallowed.

However, we usually went through the winters with nothing more serious than the odd head cold. Although we had the various childhood diseases, with the exception of one winter, I don't recall we were ever too sick with any of them. But that winter we noticed Audrey developing a severe cough and, within days, it worked its way down through the five of us until we were all heaving and choking as if each breath was our last.

I can remember the feeling of panic, as every morning I was sure I would never see another day. We were not able to go to school as Mother was sure we had all contracted pneumonia. But it didn't occur to anyone to call in old Dr. Murphy from Renfrew — not while we had a neighbour like Mrs. Beam, who was knowledgeable in the diseases of the day and their treatment.

So Mrs. Beam was sent for. She was a German neighbour — as big as a house, with a heart to match — and, according to everyone who lived for miles around, she was the next best thing to the family doctor. She delivered babies, treated colds, and cured the spring runs, so it was inevitable that she would be called in for consultation. Only if she determined we were on the brink of death would Dr. Murphy be summoned.

We were all crammed into the big bedroom at the top of the stairs. It was really a large hall that normally slept my sister and me. Mother reasoned that if she was going to have to bed-nurse the lot of us, she might just as well save herself a few steps in the process. So the cots were moved in from the boys' rooms, and the five of us were bedded down like soldiers in a barracks.

Mrs. Beam arrived early one morning. We could hear her puffing up the stairs, and we watched as she emerged from the stairwell panting for breath and as red as a beet. She had a perfectly round face, with short-cropped grey hair parted in the middle and held off her face by two long silver bobby pins. I always thought she was born without a neck because she was so fat that her head appeared to be sitting right on her collarbone.

But she was the jolliest person we knew and we liked her very much, except when she gave my mother instructions and cures for treating our various ailments that would be used only in torture chambers today. So we trembled slightly when Mrs. Beam boomed into the room and placed a pudgy hand on each forehead, telling us to cough. It took her about two minutes to determine that we had whooping cough and she informed Mother that we would be in bed for four weeks. My brothers were delighted but I started to cry, which brought on another spasm of coughing.

She ordered my mother to boil a pot of onions — all Mrs. Beam's cures revolved around onions — and once my sister said she knew for a fact that Mrs. Beam rubbed each newborn baby she delivered with onions from head to toe, although we were never able to confirm this. When the onions were brought upstairs in a large pot, we took turns sitting around it with a sheet over our heads while we inhaled the fumes. This invariably caused another attack and, as we vowed we were dying, Mother beamed saying to cough was to rid ourselves of the disease. We couldn't follow the reasoning at all.

The bedroom was full of onions, all by order of Mrs. Beam. They were cut in two on the dresser, they sat in piles beside the bed, and the mustard plasters which turned our chests scarlet had slices of onion imbedded in the mixture.

Mrs. Beam checked on us daily, puffing up the stairs and looking to make sure the onions were all in place. We thought of rebelling, determining that the disease was better than the cure, but Audrey insisted she knew children who had gone blind because they defied their elders and we weren't about to add that to our woes. Mrs. Beam also told my mother to dispense with the Saturday night baths for the duration of our confinement, but each day we were washcloth-wiped from head to toe, although Mrs. Beam would have heartily disapproved had she known.

Almost four weeks to the day, as Mrs. Beam predicted, the coughing spasms ceased. It was with a great sense of relief and thanksgiving that we discontinued the onion treatment, although the room smelled of onions for the rest of the winter. Mrs. Beam's treatment earned her the title of the onion lady, but we only called her that when we were out of earshot of any adult. We didn't want to risk going blind.

RONNY MEETS
THE TRAIN ENGINEER

My cousin Ronny was fascinated with trains. He spent hours on his belly in the long grass which grew along the tracks watching them as they snaked through our big back field close to the Bonnechere River. We could hear the steam engine coming long before it reached our property, so he had ample time to run from the barns to the spot with the best view. He rarely missed a train going by.

The rest of us would wave at Tom the engineer, but Ronny kept hidden. I thought it was just another of his idiocyncrasies — goodness knows he had plenty of those — but Ronny was plotting ways to add excitement to his life. One day, long before the train was due, he sneaked to the tracks and place three large spikes across the rails. Then he positioned himself in the long grass and waited. He had dragged me into his confidence for this experiment, and when Tom had taken his train way beyond the west field, Ronny and I tore to the spot where the spikes had been. There they were, just as Ronny predicted, flat as boards. The exercise seemed harmless enough, but I underestimated Ronny when I assumed he would be content with flattening nails.

His next experiment involved a small pumpkin which he hid under his windbreaker, making his body misshapen and lopsided as he lugged it down to the tracks. It was a small one, but it stood out like a beacon with its bright orange colour. As the train rounded the corner we could see Tom leaning out the engineer's window ready to wave at anyone who was visible.

Ronny and I were hidden from view, but Tom couldn't miss seeing the pumpkin. He must have known it was a childish prank, because the train didn't slow down a fraction as the big steel wheels hit it, sending fragments right over to where Ronny and I were stretched out in the grass.

Ronny slammed his fist into the palm of his hand. "Great," he said, "now we're ready for the final experiment." I was apprehensive but Ronny would say nothing more than "Just wait and see."

The next day he was prancing around like a spring colt, and he dragged me behind the silo to tell me to get ready for some real fun. Back then you could set your watch by the trains, and Ronny knew it was just minutes away. He ran through the garden at the back of the barns and, never slowing down long enough to spit, grabbed the old scarecrow from the middle of it and headed for the tracks. I was in hot pursuit, but could barely keep up to him.

He spread the scarecrow across the tracks, being careful to place my father's old straw hat at just the right angle so that it looked as if someone had collapsed. I didn't like the look of things. Spikes and pumpkins were one thing, but a scarecrow which looked like a real live body was going a bit too far. If Ronny heard my protests he said nothing and, when the thing was exactly as he wanted it, he dragged me into the long grass where we took our positions to wait for the train.

Too soon we heard the whistle at the Admaston crossing. We could see Tom leaning out the window looking down the tracks ahead of him. Then he saw the scarecrow. We heard the brakes screeching and the sparks flew as Tom tried to bring the big steel monster to a halt. He stopped a few yards from the scarecrow and was out of the cabin in a flash.

I blew our cover by heading for the barn as fast as my legs could carry me, leaving Ronny to take his medicine. Tom was into the long grass in a flash and had Ronny by the scruff of the neck. Chancing a look over my shoulder, I saw Ronny being shaken by the big burly engineer and saw Tom's huge hand connecting with Ronny's behind. You could hear the smacks right back to the silo where I ran to hide.

Tom took the scarecrow, tossed it in Ronny's direction and pointed to the barns, yelling, "Now git." Then he climbed back into the cab and the train took off, gathering speed as it went. Ronny took forever to walk back to the barnyard dragging the scarecrow with him.

I thought he would at least be contrite, but his first comment when he met me at the silo was, "I wonder what would happen to a bag of oats if the train ran over it." Grandma Hines used to say: "There's just some folks you can't do a thing with. You can larn them and larn them, but they never will be any smarter." I secretly wondered if Ronny was one of them.

THE NEW PRIVY

M other never liked where the privy sat. She said it was too far away from the house and it was no wonder the children were frightened out of their wits to go out to it alone at night. Father said it was the best place for it. The ground was flat, it was well away from the buildings and, besides, it had served four generations of Hanemans; as far as he was concerned, the privy was perfectly fine.

But Mother harped long enough that Father finally said he would do something about it. That meant bringing old Charlie to the farm for a consultation. Charlie was the privy expert in our area. When one got a slant that no one could right, Charlie was called; before you constructed a new one, Charlie was consulted. No one ever knew what made Charlie an expert, except it was common knowledge that he constructed a bevelled seat that was something special.

So one day after school we saw Charlie's car pulled up next to the house and we knew that a new privy was in the negotiation stage. He looked over the site Mother had chosen and circled the rock pile several times before making a comment. He held up his thumb at arm's length, squinted a bit and barely missed my leg with a well-aimed mouthful of tobacco spit. ''Yes, this will do fine,'' he said. Father's face was like a black cloud under his straw hat, and he shook his head in silent disapproval. Although Charlie was supposed to be the expert, all through supper that night Father kept muttering, ''It will never work, you can't build a privy on a rock pile.''

Before we set off for school the next morning, old Charlie was already in the yard with the pile of new lumber. The sun was beating down and it looked like another scorcher. Charlie grunted under the weight of the boards as he unloaded them from the wagon and dragged them to the site. Mother was as excited as she would have been over a new dress, and when we left for school she was standing in the back yard beaming. Father vanished right after breakfast mumbling that it didn't matter how old some people got, they just never did get smarter.

When we got to school we told everybody about the new privy. "Is old Charlie building it?" was the question of the day. "You bet he is," Emerson said proudly. "Then it'll be done right," Cecil Briscoe said with an air of authority.

There was no dallying on the way home from school that night. When we got to the back yard, the smell of newly sawn lumber filled the air, and there it stood in all its glory — almost completed. Charlie was just putting the finishing touches to the floor boards, and it looked like all that was left to do was the roof and the door. We wondered if he would finish before he went home, but with the look of the black clouds rolling in over the sky, we knew he was going to have to call a halt soon.

Over supper Mother talked about painting it green. She said it would blend in with the trees that stood beside it. "Ya, especially in the winter, when they're as bare as a skinned rabbit," Father said with more malice than I had heard in a long time. "Well, I'll tell you one thing for sure, Albert Haneman, it's going to be painted. I just hate those privies that have been left to the devices of the weather. They look just terrible, like no one had any pride," Mother said.

"Not going to matter much anyway," Father said. "The thing won't be standing a month. I'll tell you, you can't build a privy on a rock pile." By this time the rain and wind were pelting the old log house with a great force, and we all had to content ourselves with viewing the privy through the window in the back summer kitchen.

We went to bed that night and the two upstairs bedrooms were filled with talk of Charlie's new privy. The lightning crackled and the thunder roared, and the brothers, who had no fear of a storm, stood at the hall window waiting for flashes to fill the sky so they could see the privy just one more time before they fell asleep. Emerson said it shone like a pie plate when the lightning blazed.

The next morning, before we even got into our clothes, we tore to the window to see how the privy had weathered the storm. There it was laying on its side, with the two holes looking like a pair of eyeglasses through which we could see clear over to Alex Thom's barns.

When we raced downstairs, Father was sitting at the kitchen table muttering, "I said it wouldn't work. You can't build a privy on a rock pile." Mother said if he said that one more time, she was going to hit him with the tea pot.

Charlie was in the yard before we finished breakfast. He circled the privy like a bantam rooster, occasionally stopping to kick it with his boot. He and Father talked quietly under the maple tree for a while and then we saw Father go to the barn and come back with our horse, King, hitched to the stone boat. It took all their strength to roll the outhouse onto it, and then Father slapped King's flanks with the reins, and the whole thing moved toward the old privy.

It didn't take them long to right it. When we left for school, Father and old Charlie were balancing the corners with big flat rocks to make it solid.

We ran all the way home from school that night and, when we got into the back yard, there it was, with the door hung and the roof on — brand spanking new — and a scant foot from where the old privy had stood for four generations.

THE TALENT SHOW

I ranted and roared for three days when I found out that my mother had entered me in the local talent show in Renfrew. I was used to performing in the kitchen while Mother played the harmonica, but I certainly never fancied myself an entertainer. The last Renfrew talent show seemed like it could have gone right on to Broadway, and I definitely wasn't in that class. I knew how to step dance and do the highland fling but, although I was called on at the Saturday night house dances, so were other youngsters in the community. The more I thought of that great yawning stage in Renfrew, the more panic-stricken I became.

But Mother would hear none of my concerns. I was going to perform and that's all there was to it. She spent days pouring over a monologue that I was to recite. I begged her to let me just dance — at least I wouldn't have to open my mouth — but she just went on making corrections on the long pieces of foolscap that were to be my recitation. Then the drilling began. It had to be letter perfect. I can remember the title as if it were yesterday — ''Progress on the Farm'' it was called.

We practiced every spare moment after school, and I was hauled out of bed in the morning before anyone else was up to go over the actions she wanted me to use in the monologue. She wasn't satisfied until I had every gesture exactly the way she wanted it. I got to the point where I went to sleep at night saying the lines over and over, intermingled with prayers that I would survive the terrible ordeal that was before me.

I was almost physically ill when the night of the amateur concert arrived. I can remember wondering if I rolled off the seat of the buggy into the ditch as if it were an accident, would it be instant death or would I just be badly bruised and have to go on stage anyway. Mother, who now knew the monologue as well as I did, gave me no peace on the ride to the theatre. We went over and over the lines. I was dressed in a borrowed kilt for the dancing, with a pair of my brother's overalls and an old straw hat for my monologue scrunched into a brown paper bag.

I stood behind the stage with the other performers, looking in dismay at the array of violins, and the girls in their organza dance costumes and polished black shoes. I had borrowed a pair of shoes from Velma Thom because hers had buckles instead of laces like mine. I watched the perfection of a young boy playing the mouth organ, which was attached by wires to his head while he plunked away on a banjo, and I got more nervous by the minute.

Mother had enough confidence for both of us. When it came my turn to dance, she pushed me out on the stage and took her position behind the curtain to play my accompaniment on her harmonica. I can't remember what kind of a reception my number received, but I do remember charging off the stage and practically collapsing in the wings. There was no time to panic though, because I was on again with that hateful monologue in just a few minutes.

There were no dressing rooms, of course, but we had few inhibitions in those days. Mother stripped me to my underwear in jig-time and pulled on the overalls and plaid shirt. She slammed the hat on top of my ringlets, put a piece of straw behind one ear and shoved me back out on the stage.

Like a robot, the words poured out of my mouth and I saw my hands flailing in the gestures that had become part of my life for the past few weeks. Miraculously, the audience thought it was funny, and I had to stop several times until the laughing died down. Mother beamed from behind the curtain. The panic left me and I was soon into the spirit of the thing, even throwing in a few gestures Mother hadn't taught me. The audience roared its approval. When it was over, I bowed like I saw the girl in the organza dance costume do. In fact, I was still bowing when someone came on stage and gently moved me behind the curtain. The audience roared the louder. I felt ten feet tall, and so light-headed I thought I was going to explode.

Needless to say, I didn't win the dance contest — the girl in the organza dress took that prize — but when it came time to announce the winner of the monologue contest, they called my name. Still in the old overalls and straw hat, I made another appearance on the stage. Again the audience roared its approval as I took the white envelope that I was sure would hold at least a ten-dollar bill. Inside was a picture of the Renfrew Woolen Mill, no doubt donated by its community conscious owners. But I was still thrilled, almost as thrilled as I was when my name appeared in the *Renfrew Mercury* the next week.

For many years after, Mother continued to write monologues and I continued to present them to anyone who would listen. It always amazed me how confident I felt on the stage when I was so timid in the schoolroom that I was too scared to ask to go to the bathroom.

OLD HERMAN'S PREDICTIONS

According to Father, it was time to call in old Herman. Herman was the man in the county who possessed untold powers. He could tell if a cow was going to have twin calves, if there was water under the ground, just when the first snow could be expected and when winter was going to end. Mother thought the man's powers were completely exaggerated. She said he was a good guesser.

Winter had gone on long enough — it was the most severe one I remembered — and Father was anxious to get out the sap buckets. In other years, the spring calves were out in the barnyard long before this, but each time it looked like we would be heading into a mild spell, the snow would hit again with all the severity it could muster.

Word spread that old Herman was coming and, on the night of his arrival, the neighbourhood men gathered in our kitchen. When we all came home from school, we made a beeline for the benches behind the old pine table where we could watch this man of wonders spin his predictions. Mother was not pleased. She banged around the stove and cupboard, shooting the odd look at Herman. He sat in a pressed back chair, still with his wide-brimmed hat on, and with a far-away look, as if he was getting ready to commune with some higher being.

We admired the way old Herman wandered into the topic of weather. "Been mighty cold," he offered. All the men agreed. Mother snorted as if to say, "We all know that, we've been here too for the past five months." If Herman sensed her annoyance, he paid no heed. He knew why he was there, and he wasn't about to be sidetracked by any interruptions.

"Yup, you've seen the last of the snow," he said through tight lips, with his eyes half closed as if he had made contact with weather spirits. Then he started talking about the foxes coming out of the bush early, and how the smoke from the chimneys was lying close to the roof, and how the fish were starting to show bubbles on the surface of the river. He emphasized that fish were great weather indicators. The men, hanging on his every word, all nodded in agreement; but old Herman was the only one who talked. He rhymed off a few more sure signs that we had seen the last of the snow and could expect the spring run-off any day, and I tingled with excitement thinking of his knowledge.

Then the session was over. Herman rose from the chair and one of the men rushed for the door to hold it wide. Mother snorted again. After he had gone, Father announced that he wouldn't be needing the long underwear any more, and he told Everett they could start moving the new calves out to the barnyard in a few days. Mother said, "Don't count on it," as she stuffed another log into the Findlay oval.

I wondered if Mother would let me leave my galoshes at home the next day — I was sure there wouldn't be a bit of snow by morning — but I decided this wasn't the best time to ask her anything about an early spring. The next morning, I bounded out of bed fully expecting to see tulips growing in the flower bed near the pump. Instead, when I looked out the window, I saw more snow than I had ever seen in Renfrew County. I could barely see the barns, the wind was howling, the big sleigh was hidden under a mound of white snow and the watering trough was just a lump in the barnyard. The water was frozen solid in the wash basin, and Mother was chuckling in the kitchen when I came downstairs.

Father had just come in from the barn chores. His winter cap had its ear lugs tied under his chin, and melted snow sat on his eyebrows. His first comment was, "Well, he can't be 100 percent all of the time."

Mother made a point of checking to see that each of us had on our long underwear. "Better drive the kids to school today — there must have been three feet of snow come down last night — that's if you can find the sleigh," she chuckled. Father insisted it wouldn't last. Old Herman just couldn't be that wrong. He bet it would all be gone in a few days, but it turned out to be the longest, coldest, most miserable winter of the 1930s.

Father just couldn't understand how Herman could be so wrong. Mother told him that any man who didn't know enough to take off his hat in someone else's house just wasn't driving with both buggy wheels on the road and, as far as she was concerned, the sooner the farmers realized that old Herman wasn't as reliable as the *Almanac*, the better. The only thing he was able to predict with deadly accuracy, according to Mother, was that every season there would be a clatch of gullible farmers ready and willing to listen to his rantings.

THE TRAIN TO THE CITY

I marvel at the mobility of our young people today. School bus trips take them far afield, special programs have them exchanging holidays with children in other countries and family vacations often take them far away from home turf. I can't help but compare those trips with excursions we had as youngsters.

Our first trip into Ottawa by train was a special day I'll always remember. I have no idea where the money came from for the tickets, but some of us travelled free because of our ages, and I don't suppose a trip by train to Ottawa was that costly back then. We wore our best clothes because Mother wanted to make awfully sure we could walk the Ottawa streets with the best of them, as she put it.

She had no special plans for the day. It was just to be a trip into the capital so that we could say we had been to the city by train. It was very important to our mother that we do things like that — trips into Renfrew to see concerts, library cards when no other country youngster for miles around had them. She never missed an opportunity to give us the same advantages children living in towns and cities had.

We were driven into Renfrew on the wagon by our father, who accepted our mother's notion with reluctance. He was a grown man running the family farm before he ever got to Ottawa!

Since we had been on the train once before, we tried to act like seasoned travellers — going to the back of the coach for little paper cups of cold water, handing over our own tickets and trying to walk up and down the aisles with the same sway we saw the conductor use.

We stopped at all the little stations along the way — Arnprior, Almonte, Carleton Place and Stittsville. Finally, we rolled into Ottawa West where about a dozen people boarded the train to go the final leg into Union Station. And then we were pulling into that marvellous building with the marble walls and the rich varnished benches. It smelled of cigar smoke, train grease and disinfectant. The porters pushed little carts and, when they saw we had no luggage, passed us by without another glance. We were overwhelmed and held tightly to each others hands in case some stranger would come and snatch us away.

Mother gave us final instructions on what to do if, by some chance, we became separated. We were to go up to any policeman, or a man dressed in a business suit carrying a briefcase, and ask for directions on how to get back to Union Station — and she pointed out the bench we were to wait on. We were to ask no one else. It seemed unlikely any of us would get separated, as we clung to each other with an attachment none of us had experienced before.

Outside, the sun was warm and we walked to the Parliament Buildings and ran on the grass. When the big clock gonged out the hour, we were terrified. It was, I think, the loudest noise I had ever heard. Then we walked down Rideau Street and gazed in the store windows at things we had never seen before in the Renfrew shops — a window full of banjoes, another full of nothing but beautiful little girls' dresses.

We passed the Chateau Laurier on our trip down Rideau and now, on our way back, Mother asked the doorman if we might go into the lobby. This was the place, she told us in a hushed voice, where the King stayed when he came to Canada. Emerson crouched down and rubbed his hands over the marble floor and I tried to picture His Royal Highness passing through the same door we had just come in and walking over the same piece of carpet our feet had just touched.

67

The back of my neck tingled at the thought of it.

We crossed the street and looked in the window of Bowles Lunch — a huge place in our estimation — and Mother told us that was where our grandfather ate when he was downtown on business. Then we walked to a small park beside the Parliament Buildings and sat on a long bench in front of a statue while Mother unpacked the home-made lunch we had been lugging all over the city. We were glad of the rest, and devoured every scrap of lunch before neatly folding the wax paper and the brown paper bags for re-use for school lunches the next week.

Then it was back to Union Station to catch the afternoon train to Renfrew. The stationmaster walked through the marble corridors calling out the train departures, and we joined the countless other bodies that squeezed through the iron gates and ended up on the right train. It seemed like a miracle to me then.

When we got off the train in Renfrew, Father was there and I remember thinking how "country" or "farm" he looked. We hadn't seen one pair of overalls in Ottawa, or a pair of gumrubbers. Even the people in the Renfrew station looked different. We five children held our heads high and walked with a swagger, imagining that few of them had travelled as we had.

We felt very privileged indeed. The depression was forgotten for the day. We were part of a select group of people — we had been to Ottawa by train.

$\mathcal{E}$MERSON'S PLUS FOURS

The large aluminum-lined tea boxes that arrived from Aunt Lizzie in Regina, filled with hand-me-down clothes, were much appreciated and necessary to our survival during the thirties, but they often created more problems than they solved. All seated around our mother in the middle of our big farm kitchen, we rarely opened a box without a glorified fight over who was to get what. There usually wasn't much in it for Audrey and me because Aunt Lizzie had two sons, but she often tucked lace hankies inside or tiny blue bottles of *Evening in Paris* perfume. The excitement of the box was there for all of us, however, and it mattered little that the bulk of the contents would be divided up between our brothers.

That was where the trouble usually started. Once Emerson and Earl almost pulled a coat apart trying to claim ownership. Often they would end up rolling on the kitchen floor locked in combat, until Mother would threaten to move the whole box out into the summer kitchen unless sanity was restored.

Then there was the time the pair of bright plaid breeks arrived. Mother called them plus fours, which we had never heard tell of before. They were bright and voluminous in the legs and looked almost brand new. Emerson demanded the breeks and, since he was the biggest of the brothers although not the oldest, it seemed reasonable enough that the breeks should be his. The only problem was that he had already claimed a lovely alpaca sweater and was, in fact, wearing it. The breeks and the sweater were obviously the two best items in the box so Mother insisted he give up the sweater. The battle raged in the kitchen until Emerson finally pulled it off and flung it in Earl's direction.

He grabbed the breeks and, as if he didn't trust anyone, sat on them while he pulled off his bibbed overalls. He stood for a minute in his long underwear, held up the breeks, then pulled his handknit socks up over the underwear and poured both chunky legs into the new plus fours. They fit him like the skin on an olive.

Then he discovered there was a zipper on the fly front. It was the very first time he had ever had a zipper on anything. The brothers' pants always closed with big flat buttons, and this wonderful new contraption gave Emerson an attitude of superiority. He was just beside himself and for the next two minutes or so, he ran the zipper up and down at a great rate. Mother finally said, "Emerson, you are going to break it, now sit down and behave yourself." Well, as he usually did, he had to have one more go at it and that was his mistake.

He said nothing but we knew he was in trouble. His round face flushed like a red apple as he tried to conceal the damage with a spread-out hand, but little escaped Mother's eye. She sighed and said, "Come here until I see what you have done." A chunk of white underwear stuck out between the teeth of the zipper, which was locked at the waist band. Mother struggled for several minutes before calling Father into the act.

He never entered into the excitement of the hand-me-down box, preferring the peace and quiet of the farthest corner of the kitchen and the pages of the *Ottawa Farm Journal*. But he came over at Mother's call, took one look at the zipper and calmly said, "Well, it looks to me like you've got two choices — you can either wear them until they fall off you, or your mother can cut the pants off you with the scissors."

"Don't be ridiculous, Albert," my mother said. Emerson insisted he was starting to choke, but none of us could understand how he could choke from a pair of locked-on breeks. Mother struggled for another half hour or so until Father's second suggestion began to look more and more like the only way out of the dilemma. The zipper was heavy and no amount of pulling on the tab would loosen its hold on the underwear. Finally, she said in a resigned voice, "Emerson, get up on the table and lie down."

Audrey and I snickered at the sight of our oversized brother laying stretched out on the old pine table in his new breeks, the wool socks pulled up to his knees, and his big laced boots pointed toward the ceiling. Mother fetched the scissors and, with a painful look on her face at the thought of a new pair of breeks being ruined, cut into the bright plaid. She had to cut a chunk out of the drawers too. We surveyed the ruined pants as Emerson climbed back into his overalls.

Before he had the bib hooked up, he was demanding the alpaca sweater back from Earl. Of course, that caused another fight but Earl was no match for Emerson. He took the sweater off Earl's back as easily as you'd peel a banana and they both went down screaming. Mother was already pulling the box into the summer kitchen, carrying out her threat that until we all acted like civilized human beings that was where the box was staying.

As long as we lived on the farm, Aunt Lizzie continued to augment our meagre wardrobes with her sons' cast-off clothes. The battles over ownership and the numerous calamities surrounding the hand-me-down boxes were as much a ritual of those depression years as porridge for breakfast and home-done haircuts.

$\mathcal{B}$AGS TO RICHES

U nderwear, pinnies and sheets made from flour bags were a symbol of the 1930s when I was growing up on the farm. Although some of the pupils at school had store-bought bloomers and vests, or perhaps wore those wonderful fleecy ones from Eaton's catalogue, the majority of us were content to wear the ones our mothers fashioned from flour bags.

Several times a year, when our underwear drawer was getting scant, or Mother thought my sister's and my hands were too idle for her liking, she would announce that it was time we went into the local flour mill to pick up a new lot of flour bags. This was a chore Mother never entrusted to Father, because experience taught her that he would grab a handful of whatever was near the top of the bin and give no mind to the printing or the condition of the bag. But to Audrey and me, what bags were chosen was of paramount importance.

Very early in our lives, Mother would enlist our help on the day we made our pilgrimage to the flour mill. We always tried to make the trip early on a Saturday morning, because we soon learned that, at the end of the week, we had a good choice and the mill was reasonably quiet; I suppose because most of the farmers did their business during the week.

So, often just after breakfast, Mother would shift our Saturday jobs to my brothers, who would look with scorn at the chores she expected them to have done by the time

we got back from town. Two brothers would be taken off
barn duties and given the job of cleaning the house from top
to bottom, churning up a batch of butter, scrubbing the pine
floors in the kitchen and preparing the vegetables for the
evening meal.

My brothers hated the days the women of the house went
into town to the flour mill and, under their breath, we could
hear snatches of conversation about girls' jobs and sissy
chores. Mother simply shut out their protests as if she was
stone deaf. A forerunner in the women's movement long
before the term was invented, she heartily endorsed switching
jobs so that the girls had stints in the barn, just as the boys
had stints in the kitchen.

Audrey and I preferred the days before the Model T when
we had to take the horse and buggy into town, because that
stretched out our day and gave us a longer spell away from
the farm. We would arrive early in the morning and Mother
would tether our horse at the load-up area of the mill. We
would be out of the buggy as if picking out flour bags was
the most important mission in our lives.

Just inside the door was a huge bin — one that had once
been used for loose grain — and on a Saturday the bin would
be overflowing with bags. The three of us would dive in,
going right to the bottom to make sure none of the better
ones was left behind. We preferred the bags that had the least
printing on them — ones that were good and large, and preferably all in one piece and not torn to shreds by some impatient employee. It helped if the bags were more square than
oblong although, I must say, coming across that perfect shape
was a rare find.

Many times during the hunt, Mother would stop us in
mid-search to hold a bag up to our fronts to see if the printing was in too prominent a place to be of much use; and when
she found one with scant writing on it, we would all rejoice.
We found the bags with ''Pride of the Valley'' and no other
message were ideal. But ''Five Roses Flour,'' although the
whitest of the lot, were so full of company messages that we
usually passed them up. The job of bleaching out the printing was tedious and the bags, at best, could be used for tea

towels or everyday bloomers. So when we saw the bright red, mammoth words we would toss the bag aside with nary a glance.

When the heap at our feet was a couple of feet high, my sister and I would fold the bags into a neat pile, and Mother would count them before going off to find the mill owner to negotiate a price. ''All in pretty good shape?'' we'd hear the owner ask. ''I've seen better bags lining our wood box,'' my mother would fire back. ''What's happened to all the good flour bags we used to buy?'' ''Well, I imagine they're right there in that pile ready to stack into your buggy,'' he'd reply.

The transaction would be getting into its final phase. The usual asking price of two bags for a nickel was expected to be waived when the buyer was taking a pile such as we were. The owner of the mill would take a stab at a price. Mother would counter-offer. He would walk over to the pile of bags, toss through them with the toe of his boot and come back with a final price, usually a nickel higher than Mother's last bid and what she expected to pay in the first place. As soon as we saw his head jerk down in an affirmative nod, we knew the deal was closed.

My sister and I would be filled with admiration for the way our mother handled business. Then we would stack the bags into the buggy and leave for home. With Audrey and Mother occupying the one seat in the buggy, I would crouch down at the dashboard with the pile of newly acquired flour bags, running my hand through the folds until they were covered with white residue. I marvelled, knowing that the bags would be magically transformed into underwear, aprons, and linens for our table and beds — all ''brand new.''

ℒEARNING TO DRIVE

I t probably would have passed like any other Sunday night
on the farm had not Emerson lamented that he hated the
thought of going to school in the morning because everyone
would be talking about the Saturday night movies. He was
convinced we were the only family in the county who didn't
make the weekly pilgrimage into town to see the usual cow-
boy picture show. Of course, that was ridiculous because,
apart from two or three families in the community, we were
all suffering from the same disease, poverty, and a Saturday
night movie was a rare treat for any of us.

On this particular Sunday night, the kitchen in the old
log house wore its familiar look. A large kettle of towels sim-
mered on the back of the stove in readiness for the Monday
morning wash and Father was on the couch in his usual position where, unless you knew better, you would say he was
laid out. His feet were together, his hands folded easily across
his chest, and the only sign of life was an occasional puff
from his pipe which sat loosely in his mouth with the bowl
resting on his bony shoulder.

Mother got out her harmonica, but she failed to interest
any of us in a singsong, and she finally placed it back in its
blue velvet box. Even Eaton's catalogue held no intrigue,
and Audrey's invitation to come and look at pictures of the
pails of Christmas candy caused not a ripple of excitement.

Emerson did what he usually did when he was exasperated and cross. He got down on his hands and knees beside

the old pine cupboard and, with a quick flip, up-ended himself. With his feet up past the wainscoting on the wall, he balanced on his head with his hands thrust deep in his pockets. I watched as his face got redder and redder and knew it would just be a matter of time until either Mother or Father lost their patience and demanded that he right himself. All the time he was muttering about our unfortunate lot in life.

Mother usually had little time for moods but that night she, too, seemed to be especially aware that people in our small rural community, which at times seemed so isolated from the rest of the county, weren't as endowed as other folks. After listening to our complaints, she suddenly asked a question that had Emerson abandon his position, Audrey slam shut the Eaton's catalogue and the rest of us dance around the kitchen like young antelope. "How would each of you like to take a turn at driving the car?"

Father opened one eye and then the other, and I could see the pipe emit great puffs of smoke. "Are you daft woman?" he asked. "Sure it's the middle of the night. Besides, they know nothing about running the car."

"Now Albert," my mother said in her voice that told us there was no use arguing with her. "I'll be right beside whoever is driving and we'll just go to the end of the lane and back. It'll give us all something to do."

"I can think of plenty to do, if it's something to do you're after," Father said. But we all knew he had lost the battle.

We tore out of the house with the lantern casting eerie shadows in the yard, and we stood well back as Mother backed the old Model T out of the drive shed and turned in a huge arc on the lawn. "Now, just one at a time. We'll start with the youngest — that's you, Mary — but Everett you better light the headlamps first."

I climbed into the front seat and Mother, with her hands on the steering wheel to guide me, pulled down the gas lever. I was astonished and thrilled to see the car slip through the gate and head out the lane. When we were clear of obstacles like the barn and the mail box, Mother took her hands off the wheel and I navigated on my own to the end of the lane. We quickly traded places while she made a U-turn, and then I steered the car back toward the light that was shining like a beacon in the yard.

When I turned the old car into the driveway, the rest of the kids were jumping up and down making such a racket that I'm sure the neighbours a mile away could hear them. Then it was Earl's turn, and so on down the line until we all had a go at driving the car. Once I thought I could see Father's outline in the upstairs bedroom window but I made no mention of it. None of us offered to drive the car into the car shed; Mother climbed behind the wheel and the Model T slipped into its home quietly and easily.

We went into the house and the kitchen was empty. Father had vacated the couch and gone to bed, no doubt wondering what the world was coming to. But for us the exercise was a far more exciting experience than a trip to the picture show, and we couldn't wait to get to school on Monday morning to tell everyone how we spent Sunday night.

$\mathcal{T}$HE SUBSTITUTE TEACHER

All of us who went to the local school had a healthy respect for the teacher, Miss Crosby. None of us would dare cross her because, back then, the teacher ruled with a steel glove.

One spring Miss Crosby suddenly took ill, and was rushed to the hospital where it was decided her appendix had to come out. In those days the operation was considered major surgery and she was to be away from school for several weeks. However, we were not to have a holiday.

There, standing in the doorway when we arrived on Monday morning, was a young thing who looked to be not much older than the pupils in the Entrance class, and not as big as many of us in the junior grades. She seemed like a meek one all right; after she rang the nine o'clock bell, she almost crept up to the desk. In a soft voice, she read from the bible and led us in the Lord's Prayer, and then proceeded to follow the long list of instructions Miss Crosby had written out on a sheet of foolscap.

Recess came; and as soon as we were outside Cecil, the terror of the school, called us all over to the back fence for a quick conference. He said things were going too smoothly, and it would only be fitting to give the new teacher a proper initiation. All the older kids agreed but no one wanted to get involved. We in the junior grades hung back, torn between excitement and fear. When no one offered to help Cecil, he yelled, "You're all yeller. . .scared of yer own shadows." He decided to initiate the new teacher himself, which suited the rest of us just fine.

When recess was over and we were back in our seats, Cecil raised his hand. After looking over the list of names before her, the teacher said in her small voice, "Yes, Cecil, what is it?" Cecil lumbered out of his seat; "Please miss, since you're new and all, I thought I'd tell you that on Mondays Miss Crosby lets us out at two o'clock."

We saw the new teacher take a hurried look at the foolscap sheet in front of her. "There's nothing here from Miss Crosby," she said. "Well, you can take my word for it, that's what happens on Mondays," Cecil said. I could hear his toes cracking in his gumrubbers and, as he always did when he was feeling sure of himself, he wriggled his ears — which no one could miss seeing, since they stood out from the side of his head like ironed cabbage leaves.

The teacher wasn't buying his story. "Well, thank you Cecil," she said, "but today, I think we'll stay until four." She was ready to dismiss the issue but Cecil was a persistant critter. "We always get out at two on Mondays, and I don't see why we can't today." He towered over the mite of a teacher who, by this time, had come down from the front of the room with the Scott's Hardware yardstick in her hand. Still in the tiny voice, she calmly pointed out that Miss Crosby was not here today and that everyone would stay until four. She looked scared half out of her wits, I thought. Cecil was ready to go around again. All he got out was "Well now, Miss. . . ."

She raised the yardstick high in the air and brought it crashing down on the top of Cecil's desk, missing him by a hairsbreadth. Splinters flew in every direction, some landing on the window ledge twenty paces away. Cecil fell back into his seat like he had been struck by lightning. Still never raising her voice, she asked "Now are there any more questions?" We all heard a faint "no ma'am" from Cecil.

The meek little teacher returned to her desk, and when I dared look up I saw a faint smile on her lips. I chanced a look in Cecil's direction. He was down on the floor on his hands and knees, picking up the remains of the Scott's Hardware yardstick.

$\mathcal{S}$PRINGING THE TRAP

It snowed all day Friday and when we walked home from school it was like stepping into knee–high feathers. Mother let us play outside after our chores in the barn, and in the light of the lantern hanging on a nail outside the back door, we made big wheels in the snow and played tag around them. When we got to the supper table, our bodies were weary and our cheeks were burning from the cold. It was a wonderful day and I felt the contentment which always swept over me when we had fun and then settled down around the big pine table in the kitchen for our supper.

The feeling of contentment was swept away in an instant when Father announced to my three brothers that the next morning would be an ideal time to set out the rabbit snares, since their marks would be fresh in the snow making it easy to determine their paths. My stomach churned, and I no longer had an appetite for the big platter of pork chops and creamed potatoes sitting in front of me. I stole a look at Audrey and saw that her fork, too, had been laid to rest at the side of her plate.

I knew snaring rabbits was something my brothers did every winter, but the feeling of horror at the thought never lessened for Audrey or me as the years went on. The very idea of setting out wire snares for those beautiful animals churned my stomach and filled my heart with anguish. Any protest from Audrey or me fell on deaf ears, but Mother's condoning of the act made me wonder if she had any heart.

She tried to explain that rabbit meat was just the same as chicken or pork or a roast of beef, which she reminded me I ate with great gusto, but somehow her explanation did nothing to quell the repulsion I felt every time I thought of rabbit stew.

Audrey and I climbed the stairs that night with heavy hearts as we listened to the brothers make plans to get up especially early so they could cut the thin wires in proper lengths and save time in the bush while on their murderous mission. My sister and I said not a word as we settled into the feather mattress but sleep was the farthest thing from our minds. Then Audrey leaned over to my side of the bed and whispered a plan into my ear. It sounded like it would work, and I drifted off to sleep with pictures of snow white rabbits snickering behind every tree that held a snare.

The next morning our brothers set off after chores with wire clippers and a handful of various lengths of fine wire. Audrey and I waited for a suitable time to elapse before telling Mother we were going to the barn. In the distance, we could see the boys circling the bush and then disappearing into it. Audrey and I fell into step, trying to put our feet in the imprints they had made in the fresh snow and, like two sly foxes, followed their marks right to the first snare. We worked quickly, each of us undoing an end and scrunching the wire into a soft ball before pitching it as far as our strength would allow. We stayed several hundred yards behind our brothers, and talked only in soft whispers behind mitt-covered hands. The soft snow served the dual purpose of giving us an accurate map of their route and cushioning our steps so that we made not a sound.

When they finished their murderous mission, they cut across the field to the barns, waist deep in the snow; but Audrey and I waited until they were out of sight and then came back by the same route we had gone out on, putting our feet in the holes as best we could. We came into the house for our Saturday chores long before our brothers finished their barn work and we worked with light hearts exchanging knowing looks of satisfaction.

Neither Audrey nor I thought or cared about the consequences of our mission. We decided in the bush that if we had to lie about it we would, although neither of us was very good at it. We knew that, when the next snowfall came, our brothers would be back out with more snares and a new surge of murder in their hearts; but we would deal with that issue when it presented itself.

When we all gathered at the dinner table at noon, my brothers were full of comments on the rabbit snares — how easy it was to see the rabbit tracks in the fresh snow, and how they could hardly wait for the next morning to see what their efforts had netted them. Audrey and I sat across the table from each other and, stretching out our legs so our stockinged feet met in silent communion, we dug into the chicken stew with relish.

THE NEW HAT

T he minister's wife was as quiet and mouselike as her husband was boisterous and dominant, but we children were fascinated by her. Although she rarely spoke, especially if her husband was around, we were sure she just gave up trying to get a word in edgewise. We felt there just had to be another side to her that nobody saw.

She was always in place in the very front pew of the church when we came in on Sunday morning; and she sat across the aisle from us, in the curved seat, where we could get a good look at her. She never glanced left or right, but seemed to have her eyes fixed to a spot in the centre of the pulpit. The only time we saw her look someplace else was when she was following the words in the hymn book. In the winter, she wore a grey coat with a black felt hat, and in the summer, a grey chambray dress with a black straw hat. As long as we went to the Lutheran church we never saw her in anything other than those two outfits. That is until the Easter that brings back a rush of memories that gives the minister's wife a special place in my recollections.

We knew the minister's stipend was as low as the teacher's, and we came to accept that our farm community would help them both survive any way we could. The minister, while on a pastoral call, always managed to time the visit so that it would coincide with supper — and, of course, he always went home with a shoe box of eggs or a slab of headcheese. My mother, who gave away as much as we ate, would comment on the lot of the minister and his poor wife, whom she likened to a saint. Many times we would hear Mother say the poor soul hadn't had a new dress for years. My father, who thought the minister was no better or worse off than any of the rest of us, would hasten to remind her that none of us had had much new for years. Mother always ignored him.

You can imagine our great surprise when we walked into church on Easter morning and there, across from us in the front pew, was our minister's wife in the prettiest hat I had ever seen. It was a wide-brimmed hat with an array of cascading flowers in the softest shades of pink, and it looked like just a gentle touch would cause the petals to flutter to the floor. Her face wore the same look of concentration and she was still preoccupied with a spot on the centre of the pulpit, but her cheeks were rosy under the hat and my sister Audrey, who was astounded at the transformation, insisted she had on a dash of rouge. Mother poked us both on the knees and told us to hush and save our talking for after church.

When the service was over, clatches of the farming community congregated on the church steps for their once-a-week visit. As the minister's wife came out, several of the ladies commented on the lovely hat and she shyly whispered an embarrassed "thank you." Audrey, who was very conscious of our hand-me-down Sunday clothes, wondered how she could afford a hat that would probably cost three dollars. Mother was remarkably quiet; her only comment was that she thought it looked lovely.

Several weeks later, the minister came into our lane in his buggy with the dapple grey horse and, clutched in his hand with his worn bible, was a parcel wrapped in tissue-paper. He asked for Mother but she was back in the potato field where she and Father had gone to get the earth ready for the spring planting. He looked over the lot of us and, deciding against wasting a pastoral call, handed us the tissue-wrapped parcel, saying to give it to our mother when she got back to the house. He was barely out of the gate when

Audrey and I unfolded the tissue and saw inside a pair of hand-embroidered pillow slips made from well bleached flour bags.

There was a note addressed to Mother, without an envelope, and Audrey read it aloud. It was a thank-you note for the Easter hat. The minister's wife said she had never had a new hat since she had been married, and she knew that Mother had to probably sell some farm produce in order to pay for it — and that she would respect her wishes to keep the secret just between the two of them. Audrey and I felt like we had peeked into the pages of someone's private diary, and we carefully folded the note as it had been and tucked it back inside the tissue-wrapped pillow slips. Neither of us said a word.

$\mathcal{T}$HE OVERNIGHT VISIT

I t was a very special treat to have a friend stay overnight when I was growing up on the farm, and it didn't happen so often that the novelty wore off.

Joyce was a school mate, but I always considered that she was a cut above me because her family was wealthy, at least in my eyes. After all, they lived in a brick house, and she had one of those wooden pencil boxes that operated on a swivel, where the bottom swung out revealing a compartment. I wanted one so badly, but they were expensive and out of the question.

Joyce, to me, was a wonderful girl. She was quiet and pretty with almost-white hair, pale skin with pink cheeks and enormous blue eyes. I knew my brothers thought she was the prettiest girl in the school. I wanted so badly to have her come to stay all night, but I was terrified to ask her in case she said no. One day I got up the courage and, to my complete surprise, she said she would love to come and spend the night.

Then I went through the anguish of wondering if I had done the right thing. After all, she was an only child, and we had a large and boisterous family with brothers whose behaviour could be unpredictable. But the die was cast; I had invited her and it was too late to do anything about it.

The day she was to come home with me she came to school wearing white stockings, dressed as we did for Sunday church. I didn't even own a pair of white stockings. I worried all the way home that we would have salt pork for supper — I was sure her family never ate salt pork — and was relieved to smell my mother's wonderful pot roast when I walked in the house with Joyce. I saw fresh lemon pies sitting on the lid of the reservoir at the back of the stove, but one quick glance at the table revealed that Mother had made no attempt to hide the red checkered oilcloth with her white linen one. It was kept for special company like the minister, and I silently scolded myself for not asking Mother in the morning if we couldn't use it for supper just this once.

I was suddenly conscious of everything in our house that pointed out our poverty — the wash basin on the bench, the pegs on the wall by the back door for our coats, the coal oil lamps that had already been lit against the evening darkness. But I was proud of my mother's cooking, and the supper went well in spite of the long Grace my father said, and the snickers from my brothers as they stole side glances at Joyce.

My mother could see no reason why things should be any different on this special night, and I saw her go to the cupboard and take out her harmonica. I watched closely for Joyce's reaction, but her sweet face revealed nothing. Then, to my dismay, Father started to play the spoons and my brothers and sister began singing all the old songs they loved with great gusto. Joyce tried to join in, but she didn't know the words because they were songs my mother had learned when she was living in New York.

The evening passed, and we were soon climbing the stairs with our mother close behind us. It was obvious there was going to be no break in the routine for a special guest. Our prayers were said every night at her knee and, as we all knelt down, Mother beckoned to Joyce to join us. She hung back for just a few seconds and then she came and quietly knelt between my sister and me.

The next thing that concerned me was the feather tickings we used for matresses and the fact that Joyce would have to share the bed with Audrey and me. I just knew there would be no feather tickings on Joyce's bed. She probably had a felt mattress like the one my parents used.

The three of us dove between the tickings and soon the warmth of the feathers penetrated our bodies. In minutes I could hear Joyce breathing rhythmically, and I knew she had fallen asleep. I lay awake for a long time, wondering what she thought of our house and its strange routines. I longed to be like her, and fell asleep thinking how lucky she was to have her nice clothes and brick house, and to be the only one in her family; how special she must feel, I thought.

The next morning, there was the usual bedlam — getting up, eating an enormous breakfast, rushing about doing up the chores, squabbling over who had forgotten to turn the galoshes down to dry out behind the stove. Joyce watched the confusion and said nothing; inwardly I thought, ''She'll never come back to this crazy house.''

We were almost to the end of the lane on our way to school before she said a word. Then she stopped and said something I will never forget. She said, ''Mary, you are the luckiest girl I know. You have such a happy family, and your mother is so clever to be able to play the harmonica. You don't know what it's like to be the only child in the family.'' I thought she was going to cry. Then she continued, ''I've never had such a good time. Can I come back again soon?''

For an answer, I reached out and grabbed her hands. I felt ten feet tall. ''Sure you can come back. Come on, I'll race you to the end of the lane.'' My heart was light and I felt like my feet had wings as the two of us flew down the lane together — my friend Joyce and I.

THE BICYCLE ENDURANCE RUN

I t would never have occurred to my brothers to take our old
bicycle to school had not Father decided that Old Harry,
the horse we used on days when the weather was very bad,
was no longer up to the trip. Old Harry had developed the
heaves and was left to graze in the pasture in peace until his
time came.

Old Harry was only called upon about three times in an
entire school year. Nonetheless, the fact that he was removed
from service planted the idea in my brothers' minds that the
bicycle, which was almost as decrepit as Old Harry, should
be put to use.

The day my two older brothers decided to ride the three-
and-a-half miles to school was a wet fall one and patches of
water lay in the road like small ponds. Audrey and I said
riding the bicycle to school was the craziest thing we had
ever heard of — neither of us thought it would ever make
it. It was tied together with wire and bits of binder twine;
good grace and our father's patient hand was the only thing
that kept it running.

My mother tried to tell them at breakfast that they should
reconsider. At the same time, she was a firm believer in let-
ting everyone learn from his own mistakes. Certainly there
was no doubt in the rest of our minds that the brothers were
making a mistake.

At first they were going to take turns — one would ride
while the other ran beside — but there was such a hullaba-

loo about who was going to ride first that they finally decided that one would ride crossbar. Audrey rolled her eyes as we put on our heavy rubber raincoats and pulled on our boots.

We headed out the door and saw that Emerson had tied the lunch pails to the handlebars and both boys had their book bags slung over their shoulders. Everett was sitting on the crossbar and, since our front yard was on a bit of a downhill grade, they navigated to the lane with little trouble. Soon they were out of sight behind the barns.

Audrey and I wondered if we had made a mistake — perhaps we should have exercised our right to a turn on the bike too. But we soon changed our minds when we saw them out on the road at the mailbox. Emerson had driven through a patch of water that was deeper than he anticipated and Everett was standing in it up to his ankles. Fortunately it wasn't quite deep enough to go over his gumrubbers. Audrey and I passed them with a smug look on our faces.

The next time we saw them Emerson, a huge lad, was straddling the crossbar and poor Everett, by far the slighter of the two, was beet-red in the face from his exertion. Everett was struggling valiantly to keep the two of them on the bike while he navigated the first hill. They passed Audrey and me again and Emerson yelled, "See you at school." Audrey retorted, "If Everett lives that long!"

We came to Briscoe's store to find the two bikers again. This bicycle was of the most primitive variety and had no chain guard. Poor Everett was standing straddled across the bike while Emerson was trying to cut his overalls out of the chain with his pocket knife. Audrey and I passed them again. We both thought that anyone who would get back on that bike in view of all that had happened was surely a bubble off plumb.

About a mile down the road Emerson and Everett went sailing by. The lunch pails must have worked their way loose because Everett had them tucked under his arm and his leg was bare to the knee where Emerson had cut him out of the chain. They both wore a determined look that said "nothing but a hurricane will stop us now."

The school was in sight as Audrey and I rounded the last corner of the road. Like a speck on the horizon, we could see the two boys had come to a standstill once again and within minutes we had caught up to them. Emerson sure was agitated and he was kicking the bike with his gumrubber. Everett, like the rest of us, took a wide berth when Emerson was in a rage, and was standing quite apart from the action. The front tire was as flat as a pancake. Emerson blamed Everett for being so heavy; none of us dared to point out that he was a fair weight himself. Audrey and I passed by the scene as if we had never laid eyes on them before in our lives.

We got to the school on time as we always did. Much later the brothers appeared at the door looking as if they had just returned from the front lines. It took them ages to get the grease off their hands and Everett had to sit all day with one leg bare. The lunches had fallen several times and the contents were mashed beyond recognition. The lads had had to abandon the bicycle in a clump of trees at Sealey's gate.

On the way home from school, they had to pull, drag and push the wounded bicycle the full three-and-a-half miles. Audrey and I knew better than to say "we told you so" since Emerson could be a mean one when he was mad. We carried their book bags and lunch boxes home for them, more as a safeguard than as an act of benevolence. Needless to say, it was the last time the bicycle left the yard.

THE BLUE TAFFETA DRESS

It was the first ever birthday party where I received a proper handwritten invitation. My friend Joyce invited every girl in the school, and she told us there would be a professional photographer there to record the event. We were so excited we could hardly wait until the Saturday two weeks away, and the talk was all about what we would wear for this very special party.

I had few choices. My church dress was brown and drab and belonged to Audrey long before it was handed down to me. I had school clothes, of course, but everyone had seen those. I took my concern to Mother who gave her usual long sigh, which occurred when the topic of buying something new came into the conversation. I was sure I was going to be treated to the standard sermon on the depression that preceded every denial, but Mother surprised me by saying ''I think I know what we can do.''

We both climbed the stairs and went to the old round-topped trunk which stood in the back bedroom. From folds of tissue paper inside it, she took a long, blue plaid taffeta skirt she had worn in New York. Though she found little occasion to show it off on the farm, I remember it so well. It had silver threads through it, and it rustled like magic when Mother held it up. When I knew it was to be my very first new party dress, I could barely contain myself.

Mother cut a pattern from big pieces of brown paper, sewed the pieces together with long stitches and, when the pattern was to her liking, removed the stitches and placed the pieces on the taffeta skirt. She worked on the dress for more than a week — basting and sewing, changing a dart here and a tuck there. I raced home from school every day to see what she had done while I was away, and what I finally saw was the most beautiful dress I had ever seen.

It had a wide full collar, puffed sleeves, and a dropped waist with a belt sporting a huge bow of the same material. When I tried it on, it fit perfectly; and I rustled it with my hand, revelling in the sound it made when I moved. I felt just like Princess Margaret, whose picture hung on my bedroom wall. At the time she was my favourite of the two princesses, since we were closer in age.

The day of the party I was up at dawn. Mother heated the curling tongs in the globe of the oil lamp and, when she was finished with my hair, the ringlets were like tight sausages all over my head. I put on the Mickey Mouse toy watch I got in a box of Cracker Jacks; but first I put a dab of cornstarch on my wrist to prevent the tin backing from turning my skin green. I learned that trick quite by accident one day.

Joyce met me at the door and I could see Marguerite, my only enemy in the whole school, dominating the crowd in the parlour. She had on yellow organza, but for once, I felt I was her equal.

When the photographer finally arrived we all lined up in front of the player piano. Joyce and I were at the back, with the rest of the giggling girls crouched on the floor or standing in front of us. Marguerite, of course, was front and centre tossing her golden curls to get the attention of the photographer.

He peered through his lens for a long time, and we fidgeted and giggled some more. Finally, he stopped and stood for a moment in deep concentration. Then he said, ''Would you (pointing to Marguerite) move to the back, and would that girl in the pretty blue plaid dress come up to the front.''

And that's how I appear in a large photo I still have to this day — with a wide smile and a space in the front of my mouth to show that I had lost my first baby tooth. Right behind me, with the only scowl in the picture, is Marguerite, with her arms folded defiantly across the front of her yellow dress — a perfect backdrop for my blue plaid taffeta.

MOTHER'S HERB GARDEN

O utside our old log house was a passageway which led into the cellar. It was simply a hole cut out of the earth on a slant underneath the foundation of the house, and a plain board door kept the cellar secure from the elements. Every time it rained, ground water poured down the chute and filled the cellar, and the house above smelled damp for days. To minimize the problem, the vegetable sand bins were elevated above the dirt floor, saving our winter stores from destruction.

Although the cellar had served our family's needs for generations, Mother never liked the chute. She claimed it looked unfinished. For years she badgered Father to make a small roof over it and give the outside door a bit of respectability. Besides, she said, it would be a perfect spot for a little herb garden.

That was the clincher with Father. He hated herbs and seasonings except for salt, pepper and garlic — and he said he had no intention of covering over the cellar chute for something as nonsensical as a herb garden. But of course, once Mother got an idea into her head, there was little chance of eliminating it before bringing it to fruition, and soon it became obvious that she was going to build the roof herself.

Now, it would send most men into spasms of embarrassment to see their wives engaged in something as strenuous as putting up a roof — but not Father. The closest he ever got to the job was the back door of the barn, which he took to leaning against so that he could watch the proceedings without actually becoming involved.

Mother solicited the help of all the children, and we fetched nails, saws and hammers and the abundance of odd pieces of lumber which were scattered here and there over the barnyard. Her plan was to put a slanted roof over the dugout. She took two blocks of wood and imbedded them into the earth where the chute began about five feet from the foundation of the house. Then she nailed pieces of tin to the log house, and then to the boards that were to rest on the blocks of wood. She soon changed from nails to spikes as she worked away at pieces of abandoned lumber of every size and shape. All the time, Father gave not a word of advice but continued to watch the operation from a safe distance.

The day the last spike was driven home was a day of celebration. Mother sat outside the house on a kitchen chair most of the afternoon looking at her masterpiece. Father wandered over with an expressionless face and his only comment was, "You'll have to crawl on your belly to get into the cellar now." Mother ignored him. Her herb garden was going to have to wait until spring, because it was late September by then, but at least the cellarway would have a bit of protection over the winter, she said. However, when the first fall rain hit the county, it became obvious that the little roof was a perfect vehicle for it to run off and down the chute into the cellar.

Father said it was just like having a new eavestrough. However, it was not in Mother's nature to admit readily to a mistake. She said a bit more water in the cellar would make no difference to her, and he would be blessing it instead of condemning it when the snow hit and he no longer had to shovel out the chute before anyone could go into the cellar for a pan of potatoes or carrots.

The next spring, along with the acre of vegetables, Mother planted small wooden boxes of chives and mint. Father looked at the sprouts with scorn, but the little herb garden had an unexpected benefit. We discovered the groundhogs, which used to burrow in the cellar chute all spring and summer, gave the area a wide berth. Mother reasoned they just didn't like the smell of chives and mint.

She never mentioned the wet cellar again, but we noticed that whenever she had the opportunity to tell visitors about the little roof she built, she explained the need for the herb garden, not only because herbs were marvellous for cooking, but because they were perfect for keeping the groundhogs away from the cellar chute. Soon she became an authority in our area on the growing of herbs and on the control of groundhogs.

THE FAMILY BIBLE

I t sat on the only shelf in an old pine table in the parlour. It was about seven inches thick with carved leather covers that locked together with a big steel buckle, and the leaves' edges were a shiny gold colour. It was the most important book in the house when I was growing up — the family bible.

We always had to have permission to take it off the shelf to look at it. And even then Mother examined our hands to make sure they were perfectly clean so that the pages would be unmarred by careless fingers. It took all my strength to lift it, and when I did Mother stood guard to make sure I didn't bang it down on the table and mark the fine tooled leather. I was about eight-years-old before she thought I was old enough to handle the delicate task of opening the buckle without help.

We never tired of pouring over what we found inside the bible — handwritten notes, many dating back to when my father's people came over on the boat from Germany and most of them written in German. Audrey and I would mull over these scraps of paper trying to decipher what the foreign words meant.

There were also pictures of people we had never met but knew as great aunts and great grandparents — and three-times-removed cousins — just names in a long history of old pioneer settlers in the Ottawa Valley. And if he had the time, Father would stand at our shoulder and say, "Yup, that's old Uncle Herman, a real Tartar he was.'' When we stopped at his grandfather's picture, he never failed to comment on the old man's beard, which sat on his dress-suit vest like a blanket. Father would remember how the old man held him on his knee as a young boy and placed his beard over my father's shoulder and tickled him with it. We never tired of hearing the stories.

The pictures were inside oval frames glued to the page and the faces stared out at us. My sister and I would see our father's eyes looking at us from the face of a grandparent, and I can remember how we felt a certain excitement when talking about the dead and peering into the faces in those pictures.

Inside the bible as well were many pressed flowers. Audrey and I passed over these as quickly as possible, although our brothers took special delight in handling them. They were the flowers snatched from a casket just before it was lowered into a grave, and the very thought of them sent chills up my back. Although it was no longer possible to distinguish the type of flower it had been, each had a little handwritten tag tied with heavy black thread, bearing the details of the death.

Audrey and I were much more interested in the recorded births and marriages. Our own births were there, written in our mother's handwriting. We read about the wedding ceremonies and sometimes there would be a picture of a shy young couple — she in a long lace dress with a veil that looked for all the world like a curtain, and her groom in a dress suit with a high celluloid collar and button boots.

Also in the old family bible were our report cards and school promotion certificates, but these held little interest for us. We much preferred to pour over the old pictures and certificates of special family events.

Because our mother considered the bible such a treasure and something that had to be handled with care, it wasn't the one used for our daily prayers and readings. For this purpose we had a soft, leather-bound book a fraction of the size. It showed its age; the corners were dog-eared and Mother often made notes at the side of the pages. She was especially fond of reading the Beatitudes, as was our teacher, and even though I had no idea what the words meant, Audrey and I got to calling the passages the blessed verses — of course, out of ear shot of our mother who would have considered that quite a sacrilege.

But it was the big old family bible with its pictures and special certificates that held us in rapt attention for hours. At the time, we gave little thought to the importance of the written testimonials. It is only now, so many years later, that the big brown leather book, crammed full of the history of my people, is truly appreciated.

$\mathcal{E}$MERSON AND THE CHURCH ORGANIST

The church organist was someone who could intimidate a child in the congregation by simply raising an eyebrow. When I was growing up we attended church regularly, and each Sunday we marched right up to the front where we occupied the first pew on the right side. We could reach out and touch the back of the organist, although none of us dared. A mirror on a small oak stand stood on the top of the organ, and through this she would watch the choir come up the aisle. If anyone coughed or caused even the slightest stir, we would look up at the mirror and, sure as rain, the organist would be glaring at the culprit.

She wore her hair in a tight knot at the back of her head, and I remember what she looked like from behind much better than I remember her face. She had grey bone hairpins almost as big as clothes pegs, and I always thought the back of her head was more attractive than the front. Winter and summer she dressed in heavy cotton stockings that were a bright salmon colour, and her feet were tiny, like a doll's.

These small feet enthralled me when she played the pump organ. I would watch one foot rise and the other press down in perfect rhythm. It always amazed me that she could get such volume with such tiny feet. During the sermon, when she took them off the pedals, I could see where the carpet was worn — and the worn spots were the exact size and shape of her shoes.

Emerson never liked the organist much. We were a fun-loving group and he often said she was as sour as a pickle. Because we were a large family and sat in the front pew, we were especially vulnerable to her glares, and Emerson would often try to outstare her until my mother caught him at it. Then she would reach across the legs of whoever separated her and Emerson and, never taking her eyes off the minister, would poke him sharply with her forefinger. That meant, "Stop smartly whatever you are doing to annoy the organist or you'll pay dearly when you get home."

It would be no exaggeration to say that Emerson and the lady who supplied the Sunday music were less than friendly. So you can imagine my brother's dismay when he discovered that he was going to have to share the organ bench with her for several weeks.

It happened in the dead of winter. As the poor soul was going into her back kitchen one day she fell on the ice and broke one leg, badly twisting the other. In those days it was unheard of to eliminate the organ music from the church service and the minister, who was not aware of my brother's dislike of the organist, asked him to share the bench and pump for her. Emerson was furious when my mother told the minister he would be delighted, and I can remember how the rest of us teased him unmercifully for the whole week before his debut.

That Sunday the minister told the congregation that my brother would be assisting, and we could see his ears were scarlet over his one and only Sunday shirt. Everett started to snicker when Emerson began to pump and my mother reached over and poked him on the leg; at the same time, Emerson's head shot up and he glared at him through the oak mirror.

By the time three Sundays had gone by, Emerson was quite at home on the organ bench, and he and the organist took turns glaring down at anyone who disturbed the service. He was becoming downright friendly with the old lady he had spent most of his life running into the ground. It certainly was a strange turn of events! Soon, she had only to nod her head and Emerson, looking like he had been sainted, would reach over and turn the pages of the music for her.

Before we knew it, the leg was healed and Emerson was reluctantly removed from the job. There was a strange transformation in him during the church service after that. He sat perfectly still, except for his head which moved from side-to-side to keep time with the organ music, and it was his finger which shot out to poke any of us who snickered.

The organist still glared down from the bench through the oak mirror, but when her eyes fell on Emerson they would soften, and the only smile we ever saw her part with was aimed in his direction. It was as if they both belonged to a secret club.

VISIONS OF THE COUNTY JAIL

I have no idea why Marguerite spent so much time at my house. She could not find a good word to say about our farm or anything we did. As soon as her foot hit the doorstep we listened to a steady barrage of complaints about everything from the outside privy that she was obliged to use to the way my favourite cat's eyes crossed which, according to Marguerite, made him look more than a bit off centre.

One fall Saturday Marguerite walked into our kitchen and found Father engaged in the process of bottling up a batch of home-brew. It came as no surprise when she dragged me into the corner of the room to tell me how she disapproved of this most despicable practice. Fortunately, my father was too busy with the red tubing and bottles to catch her gestures or she would have been sent packing.

Audrey and I hustled her outside, not so much to spare Marguerite, but rather to save ourselves from a potential explosion from Father which was sure to follow any criticism of his favourite pastime.

Audrey headed for the wooden platform that held the iron pump over the well and set about playing jacks. Marguerite continued with her tirade about home-brew. "My mother said it is illegal — against the law — do you know what that means, Mary Haneman?" I knew stealing and murder were against the law but it was the first time I had ever heard that making home-brew was against the law as well. "I don't believe you," I said, looking to Audrey for confirmation. "Don't pay any attention to her," Audrey said, "it's only against the law if you sell it. And Father says by the time he supplies all our uncles and friends there certainly isn't enough left for himself, let alone any to sell."

That was not going to satisfy Marguerite. "Who is to know if he is selling it or not — you wouldn't know." She was working herself into an absolute frenzy. "I'm just surprised the police haven't caught up with him. I'll tell you my father doesn't make home-brew, and he doesn't drink either."

I was amazed at how calm Audrey appeared while she continued to play jacks as if Marguerite wasn't there at all. But I was suddenly overwhelmed by a picture of my father being hauled off to the county jail. Marguerite had the uncanny ability of anticipating what I was thinking — and she further terrified me by describing the county jail in minute detail. In hindsight, I doubt that she had ever been anywhere near it, but Marguerite was not only equipped with a long tongue, she also had a vivid imagination.

"I hear they flog the prisoners, especially the ones who are in there for bad crimes. I would certainly call selling home-brew a very bad crime." Right then I hated her with every ounce in me. "And they only get porridge to eat and no one is allowed to see them — except the rats, which I understand are as big as alley cats."

I pictured poor Father lying on a dirt floor, with the rats running over his starving body. "Yes, it certainly is a serious crime," Marguerite said. "My mother said so — boy, I sure am glad my father doesn't have a still in our kitchen." Audrey roused herself from her game of jacks long enough to say, "He wouldn't dare with your mother head of the Christian Temperance Association." She spat out the words as if she was accusing the man of having no backbone which, in fact, the county knew to be the case.

I was delighted to see this very man, Marguerite's father, round the corner of our lane in his late model car. He was coming to take his daughter home from what he no doubt expected was an hour of fun and laughter. He pulled up to the back door, waved to the three of us still locked in combat on the pump platform, and then tapped lightly on the kitchen door. "Gather up your things Marguerite, I'll just be a minute. I want to say hello to Mr. Haneman."

The thought of him seeing my father in the kitchen bottling the brew threw me into a panic. Suppose he told the police? Suppose he hauled Father off to jail himself? I wondered if an ordinary farmer could make an arrest. Marguerite suggested he was probably trying to talk some sense into my father.

When she got so impatient that she could wait no longer, she headed for the house with Audrey and I close behind. I fully expected to see my father in chains when she opened the door. You can imagine my surprise — and Marguerite's disgust — when we saw *her* father in a kitchen chair tilted back against the wainscotting with a big tumbler of home-brew clutched in his hand. He wore a grin from ear to ear, which we all knew he did not get from being tickled with a feather. It was the last we heard from Marguerite about her father's unblemished virtues or the evils of home-brew.

THE THANKSGIVING LIST

T he announcement appeared in the *Renfrew Mercury*. It said a huge supper, with a talent show and a real live band, would be held in one of the halls to celebrate Thanksgiving weekend. There was to be dancing afterwards and the price was one dollar per couple, with children under twelve admitted free. It seemed to be a good deal to all of us children, especially since three of us were well under the age where we would have to pay admission.

We gave our parents no peace, but for the hundredth time our mother said it was simply impossible. The tickets might just as well have been ten dollars each for all the difference it made. There was no extra money for running into town for suppers and concerts.

We knew our mother's monologue about the depression as well as we knew our own names. Emerson muttered under his breath, "If she'd put those words to music, she'd have a hit," and he scowled and kicked whatever was in the vicinity of the toe of his boot. "I'm tired of hearing about the depression," he said; but he was careful that Mother was out of earshot, because she was apt to sit us all down and give us what Emerson called her super-special version of the dirty thirties.

We wanted to go to the Thanksgiving supper so badly, however, that we carried our pleas right into the Saturday of the big event. Finally, when it appeared that we were making no ground, Emerson kicked the back stairs door in a fit of anger and, with his hands thrust deep in his melton cloth breeks, muttered, ''Why do they call it Thanksgiving, anyway? Tell me one thing we have to be thankful for. I'll bet the Thoms are going to the supper.''

Outbursts of that kind were simply not tolerated in our household, and I waited for the swat to Emerson's ear which I was sure would be forthcoming from Mother. To my surprise, she said nothing and continued to get out the baking ingredients for the big batch of bread she produced every Saturday. No one mentioned the Thanksgiving dinner for the rest of the day.

By evening, we fell into the usual routine of our Saturday nights at home on the farm — games around the kitchen table, a sing-song with our mother on the harmonica and then the inevitable once-a-week bath, snuggled close to the Findlay oval for warmth. It appeared the Thanksgiving dinner was forgotten, as well as my brother's outburst, but I was sure it would be mentioned in our nightly prayers around Mother's knee. To my astonishment, the Lord was not asked to forgive my brother and cleanse his ungrateful heart, and it looked as if Mother was going to let the incident pass.

When we came downstairs on Thanksgiving Sunday morning, as well as the usual decorations which graced the big pine table in the kitchen — like pepper squash, small pumpkins and shiny apples from our own trees — Mother had tacked a huge piece of brown wrapping paper with printing all over it to the kitchen wall. It was the first thing that caught our eyes as we came off the landing and, of course, we all flew to it.

In large, bold print using black crayon, Mother had written across the top of the paper, ''What I have to be thankful for.'' Then she proceeded to list all the blessings that were part of our lives — like healthy bodies, enough food to eat, a happy loving family, a big farm with our own animals and pets, a car, good friends — the list went on and on.

We read it, sneaking glances at Mother who was quietly stirring the big pot of porridge on the back of the stove. I noticed Emerson shifting from one foot to the other, and I could see that his ears were very pink.

At the very bottom of the list, Mother had written a special note for Emerson alone. It said, "And you, my dear boy, can be very thankful you didn't get a good trimming for that outburst last night."

$\mathcal{A}$UNT LIZZIE'S LESSON

We thought Aunt Lizzie was very rich. After all, she lived in Regina and could afford to visit us every year which, according to Mother, was once too often. My father's sister could find little to praise in my mother, and spent most of her yearly visit recounting how hard her ancestors worked on the farm, and how they certainly didn't waste valuable time reading books from the library or lying on their backs in the sun talking about silly things like clouds that looked like steam engines. It was an utter waste of time, according to Aunt Lizzie — time better spent at weeding gardens and cleaning out chicken coops. We tried to tell her Mother did all of those things too, but very early in our lives we learned that no one argued with Aunt Lizzie.

Father was a peaceful man who always took the line of least resistance when it came to a confrontation — except with Aunt Lizzie. He couldn't abide her criticism of Mother. The summer when the whole thing came to a head was hot and humid, and Aunt Lizzie had arrived for her yearly "checkin' up on the homestead to see it hadn't slipped into the Bonnechere," as Father called it.

She wasn't long in the house when she went into her usual tirade about how hard her mother had worked on the farm and what a helpmate she was to their father. I watched Father light his pipe right in the middle of eating his supper, and I knew he was going to settle her hash once and for all. "I'll tell you what we'll do Lizzie," he said, in the most formal tone he could manage between chewing his meat and puffing furiously on his pipe. ''Why don't you get up with Mabel tomorrow morning; I'm sure she'd like some pointers on how to manage her time better.'' Mother stopped stirring the gravy in midstream. Then we saw Father give her a big wink and we knew Aunt Lizzie was being set up for the kill.

Father wakened Aunt Lizzie before the sun was up the next morning. She scurried around the kitchen as Mother prepared breakfast for ten people. She was firing orders like a sergeant but Mother was remarkably calm under the circumstances. Then it was off to the barn for the milking. Aunt Lizzie was all for taking a second cup of coffee, but Mother said it would have to wait because the separator and the milk pails had to be washed. Besides, they had to hit the garden before the sun was too hot because there was about an acre of beans to pick.

By 10 a.m., Aunt Lizzie had been hard at it for five hours and no one was showing her any mercy. She was covered with mud from the night's dew and we kids thought she staggered a bit when Mother handed her two eleven-quart baskets of beans to carry back to the house. ''Just time to stem a few of those beans before the men get in for dinner,'' Mother said as she began to bang the big aluminum kettles around on the stove. Aunt Lizzie was delighted to collapse into a chair with the porcelin basin and a paring knife.

The entire afternoon was spent pickling the beans in the hot steam of the back summer kitchen, and I will say Aunt Lizzie showed no sign of weakening. By 4 p.m., Mother asked her if she would rather peel the potatoes or start getting ready for the milking. Aunt Lizzie opted for the bag of potatoes. After supper she was hauled back out to the barn to wash the pails and the separator, and the five-gallon cans that had to be washed for the morning pickup too. It was just getting dark when the two women came into the house, and it was then we noticed that Aunt Lizzie was beginning to wilt.

Mother headed right for the old Singer sewing machine and, while our visitor flopped into the nearest chair, Mother proceeded to patch the knees of two pairs of overalls. Aunt

Lizzie practically crawled to the reservoir and filled the wash-basin with warm water. Then she went to the shelf over the bench near the back door, took down the brown bag of epsom salts and poured about a cup into the hot water. Stripping off her shoes and stockings, she popped her swollen feet into the solution and leaned back into the chair with her eyes closed. We could see Father grinning behind the newspaper.

Mother gave us younger children a quick sponge bath and we had our nightly sing-song, which Aunt Lizzie was too tired to join, before climbing the stairs to bed. We expected our visitor, as she usually did, to sit up and read until midnight; but when we were in the middle of our prayers around Mother's knee in the front bedroom, we heard her lumbering up the stairs like a woman of eighty.

The next morning there was no sign of Aunt Lizzie when we came down to breakfast, and Father said he wouldn't be a bit surprised if she was called back to Regina early. She continued to visit the homestead but she had a new respect for Mother, and never again compared her workload with that of her own mother. She was content to sit under the grape arbour with copies of the city papers, well away from the action, polishing her nails and putting her hair up in rags.

$\mathcal{B}$URIED TREASURE

R onny's face was showing the strain of exertion on a hot humid day. He had been digging a hole on the bank of the Bonnechere River for more than an hour and his face was tomato red. Ribbons of sweat were dropping from his chin onto his bare chest.

His younger brother Terry and I had elected to sit and watch from the big limb of the oak tree that had fallen into the Bonnechere years before, making a bridge over the river's narrowest part. Our toes touched the water and we were cool under the branches with no intention of getting involved in any of Ronny's harebrained ideas.

In the first place, he wouldn't tell us what he was digging for. He simply said he knew what he was doing and that Terry and I would be well advised to help. That was as good as no reason at all and, as we watched him, we speculated on what he could be up to.

We were sure it would be something no one else would think of. My cousin had long since earned the reputation of being very bright and very bad. It took many more hours than my mother cared to spend disciplining him and trying to get him to conform to the rules she layed down for the rest of her family. More often than not she failed.

Terry and I watched Ronny slam the round-nosed shovel time and again into the sand, tossing each load aside. I secretly wondered if he was planning on killing our old barn cat, Giant, and burying him on the shore. Ronny had no use for Giant who, on more than one occasion, had outsmarted him. But as the hole got deeper and deeper, it became obvious that he would soon be able to bury an elephant in it. I took another chance on asking what he was digging for. In reply, he turned a scarlet face in our direction and informed me that since Terry and I wouldn't take our turn on the shovel, we would just have to wait it out — and then we'd be sorry. "You just wait and see," he roared, after throwing a heaping shovelful of sand at us where we sat only a few feet away.

Terry and I had brought down a little paper bag of lunch, and I opened it up and took out two apples. As we munched them contentedly, Ronny took his eyes off the job long enough to glare over in our direction. His shovelling was beginning to slow down and the wet sand was caked on his body like paint. I didn't have the heart to start in on the oatmeal cookies without asking him if he wanted to stop long enough for a bite.

"Well, might as well stop for a minute. I could sure use a bigger shovel." When he was safely perched on the limb, he reached for the cookies and ate them like a starving man.

"You know, you might as well tell us what you are digging for. You'll soon be down to China anyway and besides, it's just about time to head on back to the barn for the chores," I said, hoping I could get him to let us in on what he was doing without committing ourselves to any manual labour.

"Well, I'll tell you," he said, taking on that look of mystery he was so good at. "It has to be kept a secret. If the news ever got off the farm, we wouldn't be able to handle the crowds. And there'd be police all over the place. I tell ya, I'm on to something big." His eyes were just slits, and some of the red had gone out of his face. He wiggled a bit closer to us, and turned his head around to make sure no one was hiding on the ground listening. Why anyone would come down to the river to watch Ronny dig holes was beyond me, but if he wanted to play spy that was fine.

He reached into his overall pocket and took out a dirty piece of paper that was ragged and torn. He very carefully opened it out on the oak limb between us. "Don't touch it," he roared, as I reached over. "It's hundreds of years old and is falling apart. Sitting right here in front of us is a genuine map for treasure." Terry nearly fell into the water and I was dumbfounded. "Where did you find it?"

"That doesn't matter," Ronny, who never was very fond of fine details, retorted. "It says right here to dig twelve paces from the fallen oak tree and there's the 'X' to prove it. And there's the squiggly lines to show the river bank. I tell you it has to be here somewhere. Maybe it's on the other side of the tree."

Ronny had both hands spread out flat on the paper and he wasn't giving me much opportunity to read it. Only after crossing my heart and swearing to keep the secret until my dying day was I allowed to have a look. I turned around and bent down close and there, as plain as day, was my father's handwriting.

Then I knew what the treasure map was all about. Father was going to build a fence along the old tree to keep the cows out of the grain field on the other side. He thought my brothers could do it, and he had sketched out a map to show where the fence was to be. I remembered the discussion well, and the piece of scribbler paper the instructions were written on. The reason it looked hundreds of years old was that Father had probably carried it in his pocket for months.

"Come on Terry," I said, jumping off the tree. Only when I was about fifty feet from Ronny did I dare to tell him the news. He went to the pile of dirt and kicked the sand until he was covered from head to toe. His face was beet red again. "Never mind Ronny," I yelled, as Terry and I made a bee-line for the barn. "You've just dug the first post hole for the new fence."

WHERE BABIES COME FROM

I t was hard to grow up on a farm and not come to grips with the realities of reproduction, but we gave it little thought when it came to the animals. It was something that just happened, and it mattered little to us as long as they reproduced often enough to provide us with roasts for the winter, and the henhouse continued to fill with chickens who produced eggs.

But when it came to human reproduction, we were as curious as the kids of today. The subject of sex was taboo as a topic between adults and children, and when my sister and I discussed it, it was in hushed tones and out of ear shot of our parents or brothers. Even then, Audrey was most reluctant to talk about sex, and would quickly switch to something else when I broached the subject. So it is not surprising that I developed a deep curiosity about it.

I was reasonably sure that Audrey and her best friend, Iva, spent many hours talking about the forbidden subject, so one Saturday afternoon I eavesdropped on their conversation — an event that drastically changed my life for several years.

Iva had arrived about midday for her usual visit. It always annoyed me that my mother would caution me immediately upon her arrival that I was to stay out of their way and give them some privacy; so, when the two older girls headed for the grape arbour to sit in the swing, I carefully plotted how

I could conceal myself and still hear their conversation. As unobtrusively as possible, when my mother had gone to the summer kitchen, I crawled behind the old pine table and stretched out full-length on the bench against the wall. The window was wide open, and I could hear the gentle squeak of the swing and the girls' low voices. They got right into the topic at hand. Iva asked Audrey if she knew where babies came from. There was the slightest pause, and then Audrey announced that she certainly did. "If a boy puts his hand on your knee, that's it. It's as simple as that. And if he touches both knees, it's twins."

Their conversation droned on, but I was too wrought up to hang around the kitchen bench and listen any longer. At the first opportunity, I slipped out from behind the table and went outside to swing on the barnyard gate to collect my thoughts and mull over the latest piece of knowledge.

The next Monday when we went to school I was prepared. We had a game we played, boys and girls together, where teams were chosen by making fists and calling out *one potato, two potato, three potato, four, five potato, six potato, seven potato, more.* The person who was "more" dropped out and, when the numbers were down to about four people, you lifted your knees to be counted and the same process was used until all were eliminated. Well, I took one look at those girls having their knees pounded by those big, husky school boys with their clenched fists and I ran to the outside privy to hide until the game was over. No one had to hit me over the head with a brick to drive a point home; I thought little do those girls know what is in store for them. I noticed that Audrey and Iva hung back and weren't taking part in the game either.

It was many years before I learned that it took more than a boy's hand on your knee to get you in trouble, as we called it back then. As time went on, I discovered that, although I would always consider my sister wise, there were some things about which she knew very little.

THE TRANSFORMATION

I remember the woman two concessions from our road as being sickly, as we called it back then. She was tall and gangly, and hunched a bit, so that she always looked like she would fall forward if the slightest breeze came her way. "Poor soul," I often heard Grandma Hines say. "She'll be lucky if she sees the winter." For as long as we lived on the farm, Grandma Hines predicted that woman would never see the next season.

Mother, however, was of a different opinion. She said anyone who could run to every affair held in the county, regardless of the weather, was far from death's door. Mother thought the woman was a good actress, and not only enjoyed her poor health, but also liked the attention she got from everyone who came within spitting distance of her. Father said he was inclined to agree with Mother.

The woman often came to our house for quilting bees. She would stop her buggy in the back yard and let out a shrill whistle which would penetrate the walls of the old log house. Someone would have to rush out and practically carry her out of the buggy. She never failed to tell us that if it wasn't for her dear, patient husband helping her into the seat, she'd never have made it. Then she would adjust her skirts, lean on her cane and pick her way into the house. She would go directly to the quilting frame, fall into the nearest chair, roll her eyes to the ceiling and gasp, "Thank God I made it!"

The quilters always stayed for supper, and I can remember how this sickly soul would shuffle from the quilt to the kitchen table, collapse onto the bench closest to the wall and watch everyone else scurry about putting the meal on the table. The women who quilted were completely taken in by her. They clucked over her aches and pains and waited on her hand and foot.

When it came time to eat, she forked it in like a farm hand; Father always said anyone who could pack away that much food certainly wasn't at death's door, and he was sure she must have a hollow leg where she stored it. This statement made me look at her in a new light and, every chance I got, I peeked at her matchstick legs to see if I could see anything unusual about them.

Her husband was a big, strapping farmer who indulged her every whim. When they came to the Saturday night house parties, she would take on a pathetic look and say, ''You dance, George, I'm not able.'' He would bring her a plate of sandwiches and a couple of pieces of cake and she would eat her way right through until lunch was served. Then she'd tackle those platters of food as though she hadn't eaten since the day before.

Everyone said they didn't know what George would do when he was finally relieved of the terrible burden of looking after her. He had done it so long, they said, he would be lost. So it was a great shock to the entire community when it was announced, by one long ring on the telephone, that George had died in his sleep. Everyone wondered what his poor wife would do. She would never manage, was the general concensus — and it was just a matter of time, according to Grandma Hines, until we would all be gathering to pay her our last respects too.

After the funeral, the farmers talked about how they could best help the new widow, and the women even discussed going in a day a week to tide her over until other arrangements could be made. Mother, however, insisted the widow would manage just fine.

Several days after poor George had been buried, we saw the familiar buggy drive into our yard. We waited for the whistle, but none came. Then, to our surprise, we saw the widow stride into the house without the benefit of her hickory cane. With a straight back and her head held high, she immediately started negotiating a deal for gravel from our pit to fix up her culvert. Father nearly collapsed, but Mother wore that look of "I told you so."

As far as I know, the woman lived many years after her husband's death and, at the Saturday night dances, she made up for lost time and rarely put her skirt to a chair. Everyone, of course, was thrilled with the transformation and called it a miracle. Mother called it goldbricking.

"MEN'S WORK"

We had rarely seen Father so excited. Any outburst of enthusiasm was usually reserved for days when rain fell after a long dry spell, or when turkey fair days yielded more dollars than he had expected. But that night, after reading the *Renfrew Mercury*, he was fairly dancing around the kitchen.

He had been sitting in his usual after-supper position on a straight back chair, tilted back on its hind legs, with his stockinged feet resting on the opened oven door. When he read the announcement he jumped up so quickly that the chair crashed to the floor. We kids, who were sitting around the kitchen table doing our homework, thought he had taken some sort of spell.

"By gar, here's a chance for us to make a few extra dollars. Mabel, just look at that ad." He was over to the rocking chair in one stride, thrusting the folded paper under my mother's nose. She read the ad aloud: "Men and strong boys wanted for Saturday work at Helferty's bush in Douglas. Bring your lunch and your own team. One dollar a day."

Mother made no further comment, so Father filled us in on his plan. "We have three strapping young men here and, with me, that makes four of us. Now, any way you cut it, that's four dollars a week that we wouldn't otherwise see. And there's no arguing we could sure use the money."

The idea of working cutting logs and hauling them out of Helferty's bush obviously didn't appeal to my brothers because they tackled their scribblers with an enthusiasm that we rarely saw. Mother protested that the boys were barely big enough to do farm chores, let alone do work that would break the backs of the toughest men. Then Father went into his "when I was their age" routine and the boys rolled their eyes to the ceiling.

"Well, I say we'll give it a try," he concluded. Whether it was the thought of an extra four dollars coming into the house, or whether she felt that this was one of the times she should keep her objections to herself, Mother capitulated. It was clear to all of us that, come Saturday, my three brothers and my father would be in Helferty's bush at the crack of dawn.

Of course to be ready to leave our farm at daybreak meant that they had to rise long before then in order to do the barn chores. It was a sad looking trio that gathered around the kitchen table for breakfast that first Saturday. Emerson complained of a sore back, and we had to keep prodding Everett in the ribs to keep him awake. Finally Father and the three brothers piled on the flat-bottomed sleigh and, with a lantern lit against the still black morning, they headed out the lane. The brothers were big for their age but scarcely more than boys; Father, who was slight, seemed dwarfed in comparison.

Audrey and I watched the last flicker of light as the sleigh rounded the corner at the gravel pit and faded from view. It was the longest day I think we ever put in. Mother spent most of the time between the stove and the front window. She was convinced she hadn't sent enough lunch and spent the entire day cooking enough vittles for a thrashing gang. Every time our dog let out a bark she ran to the window to see if it was because her family was coming home.

Darkness closed in around us. Audrey and I were sent to the barn to do the milking and the bedding down chores. When we came back into the house the smell of roast beef and deep apple pie filled the kitchen. The table was set but there was still no sign of Father and the brothers. It was almost bedtime when we finally heard the sleigh pull into the yard. We all rushed to the door and Mother held an oil lamp high to light the way.

Audrey and I were sent to the barn to unharness the exhausted horses with orders to throw a few handfuls of oats into their feeding troughs as well. When we came back into the house, the three brothers were sitting around the table in front of mounds of roast beef and potatoes and gravy that they were tackling as if they hadn't eaten for a week. They were all talking at once, and from the conversation it sounded as if they couldn't wait to get back into the bush next Saturday. They talked about being men, doing men's work and how the other workers treated them just like the rest of the crew.

Only then did we notice that Father was nowhere to be seen. When Audrey asked of his whereabouts Everett said, "He's gone to bed. It just plain wore him out — slept all the way home from Douglas — said he never worked so hard in his life."

Between mouthfuls of potatoes Emerson added, "Doubt if we'll get him back next Saturday — he said cuttin' logs was one thing, but cuttin' and loadin' them on the sleigh, and then drivin' them to the rail siding all on the one day was just too much like slave labour. No, I doubt if Father thinks it's such a good idea any more."

On the corner of the table were four one-dollar bills. The big strapping brothers had survived the day with no ill effects, but Father, small in comparison, was no match for them. That winter, the three boys went off every Saturday, returning home after dark, and put their three one-dollar bills on the kitchen table. Father elected to stay home and look after the chores. After all, he explained, someone had to make sure that the chores didn't fall behind. Besides, he'd had his day in the bush when he was a lad.

MOTHER TRIUMPHS
AT THE LIBRARY

We grew up believing that books opened the door to vistas beyond our farm. When there was no money to spare for extras and the bare essentials had to be cut back to the bone, Mother found some way to scratch enough pennies together so that we children would have a book tucked in with our otherwise meagre gifts at Christmas and on birthdays. To her, reading compensated for all the shortcomings that came from living on a farm far away from the advantages found only in the city, like museums, public libraries and the theatre.

As the depression grew all around us, when each day seemed to be worse than the one before, the gift of a book came less often. It was then that Mother decided that her brood would join the Renfrew public library twelve miles away.

It was a well-established fact that the town library discouraged country people from borrowing books, for many reasons. They might not be returned on time; they could be lost when taken so far away; and serving the borrowers amongst the townsfolk was probably all the overworked librarian could handle.

This did little to deter my mother, however, and one cold fall day she trooped the entire bunch of children into town to negotiate for membership cards. All five of us were excited beyond belief. We had never been to this library before although we had been taken to the one in Ottawa. On that occasion, I was awed by the rows of books and the many people who sat along tables in quiet solitude reading them. Although we couldn't take the books out then, Mother took us up and down the rows, warning us not to talk above a whisper.

So, before we set foot in the Renfrew library, we knew that complete silence was as important there as it was in church. I can remember how nervous we all were — at least the children — our mother was her usual composed and assured self. She walked us all in as if it was a perfectly natural thing to do. I was conscious of being an outsider amongst the town children who were running their hands along the bookshelves with a familiarity I was sure we would never know. There was no doubt in my mind that this time my mother had outdone herself and was attempting the impossible.

She marched right up to the desk where the librarian was sorting library cards into neat piles with a long pencil. I watched in fascination as she used the eraser part to flip through the cards. She never looked up and I thought she knew that we didn't live in town.

Then Mother said she would like memberships for all of us in the library. The librarian raised her eyes from her task and peered at each of us for what seemed like hours. Then, in a whisper that could be heard on the street outside, she asked us where we lived. As Mother told her, we kids shuffled from one foot to another; my brothers fiddled with the tweed caps in their hands and my sister and I looked at the tables of books with longing eyes.

The librarian explained to Mother in exasperated tones that they had had disastrous results when books were loaned beyond the town. She complained that many books came in late, some didn't come back at all and, because of a continually tight budget, her buying power was cut drastically, allowing her to barely meet the needs of the townspeople.

Then Mother drew herself up to her full height and began to talk about democracy, discrimination, taxes and the unfairness of the system imposed on country children. Finally she said to the librarian, who looked like she was going to burst into tears any second, "Now, my dear, can you tell these five little country children that they cannot belong to your library." At the mention of the word "little," I stole a glance at my three brothers and thought my mother had gone too far this time since there wasn't one brother who didn't tower over the librarian. Then Mother rhymed off the names of several prominent townsfolk who could supply the librarian with references if she desired.

Soon we were putting our names on our first library cards promising, too anxiously perhaps, to meet all the obligations and requirements of membership. As the woman reeled off the instructions we nodded in agreement to everything she said. By this time, a clatch of people had gathered around us waiting for her decision and I was pleased to see that the onlookers seemed as delighted as we were. We left the building in triumph, loaded down with books of every description.

From then on our mother was determined we would live up to every rule the library imposed on us. She made newspaper protectors to cover each book, and small totes out of flour bags for all of us so that our books could be kept together and carried to and from the library without harm. We abided by every rule — usually taking the books back long before they were due.

Our membership cards opened up a whole new world for us and I remember those trips to the library with great happiness. Today I still feel joy when I go into a library and run my hands along the shelves, touching the smooth jackets. I know my love of books started back in that town library many years ago.

$\mathcal{P}$AINTING THE PIPES

C leaning and painting the stove pipes in the fall was a chore we kids didn't like much. The job usually occupied a full Saturday, and there were things we would much rather be doing. But there came a time in September when the chill of the autumn days settled into the old log house; morning risings would be punctuated with yelps of anguish as our bare feet hit the floor and the feather tickings at bedtime would take ages to warm up. Then, when all the signs of fall were around us, the grand stove shuffle took place.

Mother would say, "I think it's time we brought the stove in, Albert." Each spring the Findlay oval was moved to the summer kitchen, and the network of pipes piled into the woodshed. Just a scant few feet of make-do black stove pipes were attached to the stove in the summer kitchen, and poked through a round hole in the side of the lean-to.

I remember one year well, because cousins Ronny and Terry were staying on to go to school with the rest of us. So that meant an extra pair of hands to move the brute of a stove into the winter kitchen; (Terry was too little to be of much help).

Early in the day, Mother took the dozens of pieces of stove pipe out of the wood shed and laid them out on the grass at the side of house. We younger ones were given the job of taking the broom and, as gently as possible, sweeping out the interior of the pipes. One after the other would be up-ended, tapped gently with the broom handle, and great heaps of black cinders would fall at our feet. Then our mother, or whoever she thought was capable of doing the job, would paint each pipe piece with silver paint, which we all thought was beautiful, certainly much more attractive than the black pipes we saw snaking through some of the other farm houses.

Ronny, this particular year, convinced my mother that the two of us could handily look after the pipes, from cleaning them out to painting them. The groans which were coming from the back kitchen were enough to convince Mother that she was needed inside after all. The stove weighed a ton, and it took most of the morning to inch the thing into the winter kitchen. So Mother gave her last-minute instructions to Ronny and me, warned us not to waste the paint, and disappeared into the house.

"You clean and I'll paint," Ronny offered. That certainly wasn't my idea of sharing the workload, but Ronny had a way of convincing people, and I was soon on my knees with the broom inside the stove pipes, becoming increasingly blackened from the job. Ronny was slapping the paint on with great sweeping strokes and a goodly portion was landing on the grass. I warned him about wasting paint, but he was having none of my orders. He took the cleaned pipes over to the shed where he could, he said, work in peace.

He seemed to be getting slower and slower at the job, and often I had to yell at him that another pipe was ready for painting. Finally I was finished, with a great heap of pipes before me, but Ronny didn't answer my impatient calls. In itself, that didn't surprise me — he often chose to ignore those who yelled at him — so I brushed myself off as best I could and wandered over to the shed where he had taken his operation.

It took several seconds for the impact of what greeted me to sink in. There was Ronny in the car shed, just putting the finishing touches to four of the shiniest silver fenders on a Model T I'd ever seen. I almost collapsed. I couldn't speak, and though I tried, nothing but a choking groan came out. He caught my shadow in the doorway, "Pretty nice, eh? I bet no one ever thought of painting those old fenders silver."

I agreed, I'm sure no one had, and I was equally sure it was the last thing my father had in mind for his most prized possession.

"Father will kill you, Ronny LaPointe, and don't you dare say I had a thing to do with this because I think it's the evilest thing you've ever done." And goodness knows he had done some pretty awful things over the years while visiting us on the farm. Ronny seemed unfazed by my concern and assured me Father would be thrilled. "I'll bet he will," I almost cried.

We didn't have long to wait. Father came out of the house with perspiration pouring off his forehead from the exertion of moving the stove. "Well, how did you two get along," he said as lightly as a spring rain. Then he caught sight of the silver fenders.

He stood perfectly still; he didn't even finish the final wipe he was giving his brow. Then his pipe started to bob up and down between his teeth. I hoped he realized I was covered with soot and Ronny was covered with silver paint. "Get your mother, Mary," he said so softly I could hardly hear him. I ran like lightning to the house and followed Mother back to the shed.

By this time, my three brothers and sister were standing in a half moon in the shed door, looking like spectators at a side show. Mother took one look at the car, crossed herself several times, and then bolted back to the house. There were some things she thought best handled by my father, and Ronny was one of them.

Father went up to the car. With the very tip of his little finger he touched the back fender, confirming that it was as he thought — wet paint — and then he, too, turned on his heel and charged back to the house with great strides. He slammed the door behind him, which meant all of us were to keep out. He and Mother had a lengthy conference, and we supposed they became reconciled to the fact that there wasn't one thing they could do about the silver paint. To have it re-painted at Thacker's garage was out of the question.

Ronny wasn't even punished for the deed, but that evening I caught Father looking over the top of the *Ottawa Farm*

Journal at the young culprit with a look of wonderment and rage.

We weren't the only people in the area with a Model T car, but we were the only family in all of the county with a Model T with silver fenders.

"CENTRAL"

E ven more exciting than having that wonderful invention, the telephone, installed one year in our kitchen, was the realization that we were hooked up to a magical person who was there at our beck and call — day or night — called Central. Today, she's simply the operator.

Central's real name was Lucy and, to get her to answer our call, we simply depressed a small black button on the side of the oak telephone box and rang one long whirr of the crank. She never said "operator" like they do today, but she would call every phone subscriber by name and knew everyone's ring on the entire line. We all thought she was brilliant.

She must have had the patience of Job, because it was a known fact that several old people on the line would ring Lucy just to chat. Grandma Hines, for instance, who lived on the next farm to us, would indulge in this exercise several times a day if she was left alone by the rest of the family.

If there was a fire in the community and help was needed, a long, persistant ring to Central would produce a local volunteer fire brigade. All the caller had to do was ring and yell "fire" in Lucy's ear and then slam down the receiver. No names had to be given, and no addresses.

If there was sickness on one of the area farms, sometimes all the information Lucy had to work with was a frantic call which told her no more than "Billie's sick." And in due time, old Doctor Murphy's car could be seen careening down the road in answer to the call.

Of course, if the kitchen clock ran down because someone forgot to wind it, or the local train was running a bit late, you simply rang Central, asked what time it was and set your clocks accordingly. Everyone in the community knew that Lucy never made a mistake on the time. If you had to go to the train station, you wouldn't dream of leaving the house without calling Lucy to ask if it was on time.

You never told Central that you wanted to phone long distance, you simply said you wanted to phone away. It always amazed me that, after Mother notified Lucy that we wanted to phone away, there would be Uncle Herby in Montreal on the phone. I thought Central was the most wonderful person in the county.

And she seemed to know where everyone was — Mrs. Beam had gone to Renfrew, or Mr. Briscoe was gone to the grist mill and should be back in an hour, or Alec Thom had driven the children to school. No one thought she was prying; we expected Central to know these things, and she seemed to think it was part of her job.

When people ask me what I miss most about living on the farm during the 1930s, I mention things like homemade butter, the cool delight of the ice house on a hot summer day or the smells pouring out of the smoke house. But I also miss the wonderful familiarity of that link with the outside world — Lucy, known to all as Central.

OLD CHARLIE'S DEAL

Old Charlie was a bachelor, and he looked every inch the neglected being who didn't have the deft touch of a woman's hand to mend his clothes or see to his personal needs. He was overweight by about seventy-five pounds, only shaved when the spirit moved him, and his clothes looked like they had never had close contact with a bar of soap or a needle. He drove an old Chev truck that looked as shabby as Charlie did. Pieces of rope held the door shut and the two front fenders were different colours where Charlie had attempted and failed to paint them grey with mismatched barn paint.

One Saturday Charlie arrived with the old truck and beckoned my father to come out in the yard. Farmers rarely discussed important business in the house so we knew Charlie was there to talk seriously about something. We heard him drive away and soon Father came into the house. We hadn't seen him so excited since he traded nine loads of gravel for a neighbour's old Model T Ford. It seemed Charlie was cutting down on farming by renting out most of his land; the rheumatism was bothering him and he wanted to take life a little easier. He offered Father the old Chev truck if Mother would just do up a bit of washing for him each week and maybe a spot of baking.

Right off the bat Mother emphatically said "no." She had enough laundry of her own to do and, besides, you'd never fill old Charlie because he ate like a horse. But the boys put up such a fuss, roaring like banshees, that she finally relented — but only for a week to see how the deal would work out. She would never commit herself to anything she could not finish, and she wanted a way out of this arrangement if need be.

That week Charlie delivered the truck but said he would wait until Saturday to bring the laundry. Mother brought out loaves of bread, a couple of pies, sticky buns and a jar of icicle pickles. Charlie took hold of the box with dirty hands the size of frying pans and beamed like someone had just given him a twenty-dollar bill. He moved over to the passenger side so Everett could drive him home and, before my brother got behind the wheel, Charlie had wolfed down most of the sticky buns.

It was a glorious week. The boys drove the truck into town, out to the fields, back to the gravel pit and over to the Thoms. They painted the fenders to match and threw out the old straw cushions that Mother insisted smelled too much like Charlie. That Saturday, Charlie arrived by horse and wagon with his laundry. It looked like he had moved out. There were blankets, sheets, long underwear from the winter before, and enough shirts to dress half the county. Everything was the same colour — dirty grey.

Mother looked at the mountain of laundry in anguish but, before she could do much more than nod hello, Charlie was gone and the laundry was piled on the back stoop. He was no sooner out the lane than Mother ordered all of us to help, Father included, who lamented that washing clothes was women's work. It took almost two days to work through Charlie's dirty laundry. Mother boiled the underwear in the laundry tub on the back of the stove but no amount of homemade lye soap or hot water could whiten the sheets. Audrey was terrified someone would see the underwear draped over the fence to dry and think it belonged to us.

Father didn't have to ask if the deal was off. When the laundry was finally washed and dried, he loaded it, neatly folded, into the back of the old Chev truck and ordered Everett to follow in the Model T. We all knew the truck wouldn't be making the return trip.

THE PONY AND THE CART

M arguerite, a school classmate, wasn't like the rest of us. As an only child, we all thought she was spoiled rotten. She had the first painted lunch box in the school, and the first permanent wave I had ever seen on anyone under thirty. But what distinguished her more than anything else was her underwear, which came straight out of Eaton's catalogue. Ours, of course, was made of bleached flour bags.

If she had been humble about all these special privileges, she probably wouldn't have been so resented. But her high-falluting attitude did nothing to endear her to any of us, and when she bragged about her accomplishments or possessions, we would find some fault to take the wind out of her sails.

One day the word was out that Marguerite's parents had bought her a pony and a little pony cart to go with it. None of us could imagine why she needed it, as she lived within a stone's throw from the school. "Just to show off, you can be sure," my best friend Velma said.

"As far as I'm concerned, I wouldn't take a ride in the cart if she offered it," Joyce said. "She's not likely to offer, so I wouldn't worry about it," Velma shot back, with more malice than I had ever heard come out of her mouth.

"Just selfish, that's all she is. . .plain and simple selfish," someone else threw in. "Imagine having a pony and cart, and I dare say it's the first one in the Northcote area, and not even offering any of us a ride. Well, it's what I'd expect from the likes of her."

We were all swinging on the school gate and looking toward Marguerite's house down the road. I wondered why she hadn't shown up yet. "It isn't like Miss Perfect to be late for school," I said. "Maybe the pony kicked her," Velma offered. That mental picture tickled our fancy and we all made a contribution to what we thought she would look like if she ended up being tossed into the manure pile by her new pony.

Joyce ran to the school door to look at the time on the big round clock that hung on the front wall near Miss Crosby's desk. "It's almost half past eight. She's always here by now." Finally, Velma figured the whole thing out. "She's going to come in late, driving that new pony and pony cart just to make a grand entrance. I can tell you right now, she wouldn't drive it over here if she didn't have an audience, and she's waiting until the yard is full, you can be right sure of that."

That made perfect sense to the rest of us. Then Hazel, who Velma always said had an evil strain in her blood, suggested when Marguerite arrived that not one of us cast as much as a glance in her direction. We wouldn't acknowledge the fact that she had come with a new pony and cart, or even speak to her. We all spit on the end of our thumbs and touched each other with our wet hand to seal the pact.

Then in a few minutes, as we knew she would, we saw Marguerite coming around the corner of her barn in the little cart with the grey pony at a dead trot. We got off the gate and sat on the grass in front of the school door. Marguerite would have to pass right in front of us to get to the drive shed, and Hazel gave us the final instructions on what to do when she came into the yard. We were to laugh and giggle and pretend we were involved in some sort of secret and not once, under the threat of violence after school, were we to glance in her direction.

We heard the cart leave the gravel road and enter the yard. We all took our cue from Hazel and jabbered away like magpies. We would have had to have been blind not to see Marguerite pull up right in front of us, but we ignored her admirably. Then we heard her voice rise above the chatter, and we couldn't believe our ears. "We have time before Miss Crosby rings the bell to each have a drive," she was saying. "If we go in twos, everyone will get a turn before school."

Hazel stopped in mid-giggle. Velma and I were already heading for the pony cart. None of us had any idea what had taken hold of Marguerite and none of us cared. We all had a turn around the schoolyard in the little cart, and Marguerite's store-bought underwear and promises sealed with spit on the thumb were soon forgotten.

$\mathcal{T}$HE GOBBLER'S REVENGE

For the most part, the farm livestock seemed a contented lot. They were well fed, adequately housed and generally led uncomplicated lives, unlike the farmers of those hungry thirties who carried on a never-ending struggle for survival. But I have dark memories of one of those creatures, and although it must have met the same fate all the livestock eventually did, it always seemed to be around to terrorize us.

It was a gobbler of enormous size, and not only did it rule the barnyard with a vicious superiority, it terrorized us so thoroughly that we never went out without a switch for protection if we knew it was on the loose.

It stood about two feet high without counting its long, red, rubbery neck which it could stretch out another foot when the spirit moved it. It was fat, too, probably because it ate its share of feed as well as that of most of the flock. The turkeys would cower in the corner of the yard until the old gobbler moved away from the feeder. Only then would they dare venture over to the grain. Its eyes never missed a trick and it seemed to sense immediately when someone came within fifty yards of the barnyard. It would come gobbling out of hiding and lunge at us, sending us into hysterics as we charged for the hayloft ladder or the gate as fast as our legs could carry us.

It didn't help matters a bit that Emerson taunted the bird every chance he got — from the safety of the closed gate, of course. Emerson would rattle a stick of wood between the rail fence, make a reasonable facsimile of a gobbler's noise, and the big bird would roar out from wherever it was hiding and run headlong into the rails. Emerson would work the bird into such a frenzy that it would be beside itself with rage, but the only thing it could do was lunge for the other turkeys and send them scurrying for cover.

Of all of us, the gobbler liked Emerson the least. It had an uncanny sense of timing, and rarely did my brother go to the barnyard that the gobbler wasn't right there to greet him. Emerson was a big, strapping chunk of a lad, but that bird with the ugly disposition was one thing he couldn't handle.

One day the gobbler finally evened the score between the two of them. Emerson had gone to the barnyard, as he said later, just to poke around. My sister and I said he likely went to aggravate the gobbler, but when he went in through the gate, the bird was nowhere in sight. As he went in the barn, however, it suddenly appeared from nowhere and blocked the doorway.

We heard the familiar gobbles of rage from the bird, and the roars from Emerson, and we charged to the fence just in time to see him take a flying leap onto the back of the first holstein he came to. The cow wasn't too pleased and showed it by kicking one leg after the other until Emerson had no choice but to jump off or be thrown to the floor.

The gobbler moved further into the barn. Emerson had less than two yards of space and the only other exit was over the manure pile at the far end of the building. To reach that little door, he had to work his way down the line of cattle through their feeding troughs. Now the cows weren't any fonder of the gobbler than we were, and they were bawling their disapproval and pulling at the straps which secured them in the stable.

We four stood safely behind the fence, powerless to help Emerson who was considering his options. At the moment, they weren't too promising. Everett yelled at him to make a charge for the door, but the gobbler opened its wings in anger and it looked doubtful if Emerson was going to risk that exit. The battle raged on for the better part of an hour with Emerson no closer to an escape than when the stand-off started.

"I guess it's over the manure pile for you," Everett yelled. Emerson looked at the gobbler and then looked at the little door out of which we shovelled the daily collection of ferti-lizer. A fresh accumulation had just been added to the heap that morning.

Emerson made his decision, and we saw him climb over the first cow's head and vanish from sight. All eyes moved to the end of the building as we waited for our brother to appear around the corner. The gobbler was still strutting across the doorway when we saw Emerson make a bee-line for the gate. He went like the wind and we were ready for him as he slid through seconds before the old gobbler real-ized he was out of the barn.

We slammed the latch behind him and took a good look at him. He was manure to the cuffs of his short overall pants and smelled something awful. But he had the common sense to take off his gumrubbers before he jumped — they were as clean as a whistle.

CARMEL THE CAT

A unt Edith was a favourite great aunt who came to visit us regularly on our farm during the thirties. We all thought she and Uncle George were very wealthy because he was an engineer, which made him a professional, and Aunt Edith owned a beauty salon. As well as that, they claimed to own one of the Thousand Islands, and had a long mahogany launch to ferry themselves between the island and their home in Gananoque.

They had no children, but had a passion for animals, and to us their main claim to fame was the huge golden cat they owned and which my father insisted was better looked after than most kids he knew. The cat was called Carmel, and Aunt Edith had a special way of saying its name that reminded me of a doting grandmother speaking softly to a child. She talked to the cat as if it was human, and I was entranced with the way she would ask the cat a question. . .or say "isn't that right Carmel?" I fully expected one day to hear the cat answer.

Mother thought all cats belonged in the barn, and as long as we lived on the farm, I never knew a cat to come into the house. Aunt Edith thought it was a crime the way we ignored the cats on the farm. She thought they should all be allowed in the house at will, and she was further appalled when she found out that, with the exception of two or three, we called them all simply *cat*.

When we got a letter to say that Aunt Edith and Uncle George were coming for a weekend, we knew Carmel would be along with them too. The minute Mother got word, she would start making plans on what to do about that fool cat, as it became known. She refused to call it by its given name, and time and again said the old couple would have been better advised to lavish their attention on the thousands of orphans in the country instead of a cat. But nothing was ever said to their faces, and so when they came with Carmel, Mother accepted the cat as another houseguest, however reluctantly.

They would drive into the yard in their big shiny Buick with suitcases strapped onto a little wire rack on the running board, so as to give Carmel more space in the car. The cat was invariably draped around Aunt Edith's neck like a huge fur collar and, from the time they stopped the car until they left, I scarcely took my eyes off the animal. To me, it was almost human.

Aunt Edith would carry it into the house as if it were a baby, and its big slanted eyes peered out at us like beacons. She would head right for the rocking chair where she would settle the cat on the fat cushion, talking to it all the time about what fun they were all going to have on the farm. Father was just disgusted with the carrying on; and little did Aunt Edith know that, in anticipation of knowing exactly what she would do with Carmel when she came into the house, Mother had already changed the chair cushion for one that was out in the driving shed and kept for just such a purpose. Heaven forbid that a cat would ever sit on one of the cushions we used in the house!

Aunt Edith always brought Carmel's own dishes with her, which suited us just fine. Had the cat ever touched a dish we ate from, the dish would have gone right into the refuse pile. Mother wouldn't even bother to wash it, so distasteful would the whole idea be to her. But Aunt Edith brought little baby dishes, one for milk and one for food, and Carmel would eat from them and only them, according to Uncle George.

The cat was thoroughly housebroken, which was a godsend, and as regular as clock work, every hour or so, Uncle George would pick Carmel out of the rocking chair and mutter that it was time to "go for our walk" as he called it. Out they would go with Uncle George chatting away to the cat as if it knew every word he was saying. Emerson said it was cat instinct that kept our own cats well away from the house when Carmel came to visit, because all the time our aunt and uncle were there, we never laid eyes on one of our own.

Father thought it was absolutely sinful the way Aunt Edith and Uncle George lavished attention on their cat. He insisted that some day they would be in dire want, and then they would know what poverty was all about. I pressured him to tell us what he meant, as I pictured Aunt Edith and Uncle George being hauled away to the poor house, but Father would only say, "you just wait and see."

However, in spite of Father's predictions that God would look with disfavour on anyone who spent so much time and money on a lowly cat, Aunt Edith and Uncle George lived to spend many weekends with us on the farm. And Carmel, that almost human cat, continued to be the centre of their lives. It seems to me now that the cat lived much longer than cats normally do, because for years it came to the farm whenever they did.

Although Mother never did like Carmel spending the weekends inside the house, she accepted it with reluctance and tolerance. She rationalized that the couple was old and the cat brought them joy and purpose. When she talked about the cat in that vein, I would often suggest that one of my favourite barn cats could perhaps be brought into the house on occasion too. Her answer was always the same. "Certainly not. Cats belong in the barn." There was no such thing in those days as negotiations between parent and child, so I knew for her the matter was closed. *Our* cats stayed in the barns.

NO ANTIQUES FOR ME

A lthough my memories of our old log house are ones of cozyness and comfort, I wonder if they are not a bit coloured by thoughts of a warm and caring family, and the ability of a young child to shut out everything but pleasant recollections. I say this because, when I look back, I see the crisp, flourbag embroidered curtains at the window and feel the warmth of the Findlay oval, but the truth is the furniture was unbelievably uncomfortable, with the exception of the wonderful soft feather mattresses which, even today, I long to return to.

Our seats at the dining table, for instance, were nothing more than two long benches on either side. Father and Mother sat on pressed back chairs at both ends, but we children sat on those backless benches as long as we lived on the farm. And a big brother, by digging his heels in the floor under the table, could silently tip the thing over, sending a small sister crashing backwards on her head. Those benches were cold and unyielding, and leaving the table in the middle of a meal meant having everyone rise to let you out. They were marvellous to hide on when the table was pushed back against the wall, but otherwise offered little comfort to those who had to use them.

There is a great clamour today for the old-fashioned breadboxes, and I suppose for those who weren't raised with them sitting adjacent to the kitchen stove, they hold a bit of intrigue. But when I think of breadboxes, all I remember is that unmistakable smell of stale yeast. It didn't matter how meticulously the thing was cleaned out each time it was used, it still smelled of yeast — so I can never understand the modern attraction of old breadboxes.

Although the Findlay oval was a marvellous development in its day, I would be loathe to return to it as my only means of cooking now. First of all, it was massive. It took up one whole end of our kitchen, and it didn't matter how careful you were, there was always a little cloud of ashes sitting on the floor around the fire box. I can remember my mother down on her hands and knees with a damp cloth wiping off the floor. . . only to have another mound of ashes accumulate by the time she rinsed out the rag. The only way to keep the top clean and shiny was by rubbing it with bacon drippings or goose grease while it was hot. When Mother was at this task everyone, including Father, cleared out of the kitchen. The stove had to be blistering hot to burn off the fat, which meant that smoke and fumes would rise off it like an erupting volcano. Only by opening the back door could we rid the kitchen of the burnt smell.

I suppose it was a blessing that families in those days had little in the way of precious linens, because there certainly was no place to store them. The back-to-the-wall cupboard was not more than twelve inches deep, and by the time the tea towels, the pinnies and the one good cloth reserved for company and Sundays were stashed in its one drawer, there was room for little else. The glass doors at the top held our best dishes — those that came free in puffed wheat bags — and the few possessions Mother considered a cut above everyday. When we took out the good dishes the cupboard was bare and, as Mother often said, when you wanted it to look its best, it looked its worst. I have a great deal of difficulty working up any warm feelings toward a back-to-the-wall cupboard.

The only time we saw clothes closets was when we visited Aunt Nellie Wagonblass in Arnprior. Every bedroom in her house had a closet and, in one bedroom, you could walk into the closet and still have room for the clothes. On our farm we hung our clothes behind the bedroom door, which meant that what you wanted to wear was usually at the bottom of the hook and every last item had to be removed before you got to it.

How marvellous it would have been if my sister and I had one of those massive, long dressers to share instead of the little washstand that stood at the head of our bed. A narrow cardboard box divided the one drawer, and the two doors at the bottom offered little space for anything more than our sweaters and long underwear.

Every kitchen I knew had a crêton-covered couch and, at the time, I thought it was a great place to curl up on a cold winter's night. But the mattress was straw, and if you wanted to take the patchwork quilt off the bottom to toss over yourself, you removed the only protection you had from the sharp straws that poked through. So, by today's standards, the old couch would be considered a hardship indeed.

At our back door was a long deacon's bench, which Father told us came out of an old church. It was made of oak and was shiny smooth from so many bottoms sitting on it over the years. This is where we sat to put on or remove our galoshes and boots, but it was next to impossible to remain seated for any length of time. As soon as your melton cloth coat hit the bench, you began to slide, until eventually you were half on and half off the thing. You could only hope that your boots were off before you hit the floor. Of course, it was bone hard and the back was as straight as a die — so that no one would slouch in church, I suppose. It was typical of the furniture of the times.

When I hear people becoming nostalgic over old breadboxes, I think of the slivers I got in my hands, and when I think of the washstands I remember the crowded interiors. Although I harbour warm memories of those days on the farm in the 1930s, I do not pine for those pieces of early Canadian furniture which filled our house. As far as I'm concerned, if I never see another deacon's bench as long as I live, it will be too soon for me.

ONE FOR SORROW, TWO FOR JOY

Summertime — that magical time in my youth has left so many joyful memories. A time when words like "depression" and "survival" were not to be worried about by children, but were to be dealt with by grown-ups who were better prepared to handle them. Like old movie frames that flash before my mind's eye, the summer pictures I harbour with a fierce protection are ones of happiness and family fun — and of customs born out of routine and sometimes desperation.

Only now can I fully appreciate how lonely our mother must have been for the city she turned her back on when she came to a primitive farm in a tight-knit rural community to raise a large family. She was miles away from everything she had grown to love — the opera, concerts, electricity, and things as simple as running water or store-bought sliced bacon. What a different life she had chosen and what a price she must have paid for that decision.

Back in the thirties when the sun warmed the earth and parched the air, turning the ground to dust, we coped with the summer heat by plunging into the cool Bonnechere water, lunching under the grape arbour, tenting in the back yard on warm nights and riding bare back on a docile horse that had nothing better to do than cater to the whims of five rambunctious farm kids.

But it was in the summers, I recall now, that Mother often quit the house, turning her back on the chores that kept her busy from dawn to dusk and escaping in body and soul from that which tied her as surely as if she had been bound with a rope.

Audrey said she always knew when Mother's thoughts would turn away to another time and place. She said she could tell because Mother would not demand perfection that day in the countless household chores Audrey and I were expected to perform. Instead, she would get that faraway look that meant her mind was someplace else.

And always that would mean we children would be hustled out of the cool confines of the old log house and invited to go with Mother to the edge of our back yard where the first grain field met the soft grass. Here, she would stretch out on her back and we would sprawl around her and play a favourite game that brings back delightful memories. We'd watch the puffed white summer clouds slide across the sky and we'd all offer comments like, ''I think it looks like a steam engine'' or, ''No, it doesn't, it has a head like a dog.'' And so the game would go on. Occasionally, Mother would smile, but more often she would follow the clouds with her eyes shaded by a hand and say nothing.

Then the blackbirds would appear, flying across our pictures, and Mother would come alive and point, ''There they are! One for sorrow, two for joy, three for a girl, four for a boy, five for silver, six for gold. . .'' and so it would go.

If we saw only one blackbird — one for sorrow — we'd frantically search the sky for one more to break the luck. Sometimes, we'd pretend a crow was a blackbird so that we could find joy, but we were only fooling ourselves. Mother, too, would be caught up in the search, and it seems to me now that it was more important to her than it was to us.

To us, the blackbirds were a game to be played in the hot summer sunlight under a blue sky. But to Mother, I think, they were a promise that, if one was for sorrow, somewhere in the clouds of that summer sky surely joy would not be far behind.